Air Fryer Cookl

1000 days of effortless and tasty recipes for newbies and pro

Table of Content

Introduction

What is an air fryer? How does it work?
The air fryer works like a more powerful countertop convection oven that does not fry food. However, we consider that there is a distinction between air-frying and baking. The small appliance claims to replicate the results of deep-frying using only hot air and rarely little or no oil.
This device's popularity has grown in recent years. There are numerous foods that can be air-fried (from frozen chicken wings and homemade french fries to roasted vegetables and fresh-baked cookies).

An air fryer's top section has a heating mechanism and a fan. When you switch the air-fryer on, hot air rushes down and around the food, which is placed in a fryer-style basket. This rapid circulation crisps the food, similar to deep-frying but without the oil.
This is how you use an air fryer:
Put your stuff in the basket.
> It can hold anywhere from 2 to 10 quarts, depending on the size of your air fryer. In most cases, a single or a couple of teaspoons of oil will be sufficient to help the food crisp up. In case that you're in a hurry, you can use foil to make cleanup easier in an air fryer.

Establish the time and temperature.
> Depending on the food, air fryer cooking times and temperatures typically range from 5 to 25 minutes at 350° to 400°F.

Allow the food to cook.
> In some cases, flipping or turning the food halfway through the cooking time may be necessary to help it crisp up evenly. It's mandatory to clean your air fryer after you've finished cooking.
> Do you want to know how to make crispy, golden-brown air-fried food? We've got air fryer tips to help every recipe turn out perfectly—as well as air fryer mistakes to avoid.

In an air fryer, what can you cook?
While many of the most delicious and popular air-fryer recipes are for deep-fried foods, this appliance can also cook meat, roast vegetables, and bake cookies.

Finger Foods from Frozen
When preparing frozen foods that are meant to taste deep-fried, the air fryer shines. Many frozen air-fried foods are available, including frozen french fries, mozzarella sticks, and chicken nuggets.

Finger Foods Made from Scratch
If you prefer to prepare your finger foods, the air fryer is a great way to make crispy homemade snacks and sides—try air-fryer sweet potato fries, air-fryer pickles, or air-fryer potato chips. Don't miss out on these addictive air-fryer appetizers, such as air-fryer ravioli and air-fryer egg rolls.
Fresh cheese melts into a gooey mess, whereas air-fried frozen mozzarella sticks are delicious (so homemade cheese curds are out).

Meat, chicken, and fish
You can make tender and juicy air fryer chicken. Try recipes for air-fried chicken, such as air-fried Nashville hot chicken. We love this air-fryer crumb-topped sole and this air-fryer cod when it comes to fish and seafood. Air-fryer keto meatballs are an excellent option for a healthier life.
This fantastic appliance can also make comforting recipes like an air-fryer meatloaf and pork loin roast.

Vegetables Roasted

Air fryers are ideal for roasting vegetables because they are essentially small conventional ovens—especially if you're only cooking for one or two people. Air-fryer herb and lemon cauliflower, red potatoes, air-fryer asparagus, and garlic-rosemary Brussels sprouts are just a few of our favorite air-fryer vegetable recipes.

However, avoid using leafy greens when using this gadget to cook vegetables.

A few baked goods

Air fryers are ideal for making single-serving desserts such as cookies and apple fritters (here's how to make air-fryer cookies). Make air-fryer peppermint lava cakes for the holidays, or air-fryer doughnut holes for an indulgent treat any time of year. Don't forget the air fryer for breakfast: air-fryer bourbon bacon cinnamon rolls and air-fryer French toast sticks are two breakfast recipes to try.

You cannot make anything that requires a liquid batter (unless you freeze it first).

Air Fryer Frequently Asked Questions

Is air-fried food nutritious?

Food cooked in an air fryer can be considered healthier than deep-fried food because it uses less oil. Frozen air-fried french fries have 4 to 6 grams of fat per serving, compared to deep-fried counterparts, which have a whopping 17 grams.

What are the pros and cons of air fryers?

Pros: Air fryers make it simple to reheat frozen foods, and they can do so in a slightly healthier way than deep-frying. The results are far superior to oven-frying, and your kitchen remains cool.

Cons: Even the biggest air fryers have a limited capacity, so you'll have to cook in batches, especially if you're cooking for a large group. Air fryers have a bigger size than a toaster and take up more counter space. Some models can be costly.

Is it worthwhile to purchase an air fryer?

With so many models on the market, the price of this popular appliance has come down in recent years (many models cost less than $200, and some cost less than $100). An air fryer is well worth the investment if you frequently prepare fried foods (frozen or homemade), reheat leftovers often, or experiment with new cooking appliances.

Breakfast

1. Cheesy Ham Egg

Preparation time: 10 minutes　　　**Cooking time:** 15 minutes　　　**Servings:** 4

Ingredients:

- 4 medium green bell peppers
- 1 tablespoon coconut oil
- 3 ounces (85 g) chopped cooked no-sugar-added ham
- ¼ cup peeled and chopped white onion
- 4 large eggs
- ½ teaspoon salt
- 1 cup shredded mild cheddar cheese

Directions:

1. Place peppers upright into ungreased air fryer basket. Drizzle each pepper with coconut oil. Divide ham and onion evenly among peppers.
2. In a medium bowl, whisk eggs, then sprinkle with salt. Pour mixture evenly into each pepper. Top each with ¼ cup cheddar.
3. Adjust the temperature to 320F (160C) and set the timer for 15 minutes.
4. Serve warm on four medium plates.

Nutrition:

Calories: 281

Fat: 18g

Protein: 18g

Carbohydrates: 8g

Fiber: 2g

2. Cheesy Roll

Preparation time: 10 minutes　　　**Cooking time:** 20 minutes　　　**Servings:** 12 rolls

Ingredients:

- 2½ cups shredded Mozzarella cheese
- 2 ounces (57 g) cream cheese, softened
- 1 cup blanched finely ground almond flour
- ½ teaspoon vanilla extract
- ½ cup Erythritol
- 1 tablespoon ground cinnamon

Directions:

1. In a large microwave-safe bowl, merge Mozzarella cheese, cream cheese, and flour. Microwave the mixture on high 90 seconds until cheese is melted.
2. Add vanilla extract and Erythritol and mix until a dough form.
3. Once the dough is cool enough, set it out into a 12-inch × 4-inch rectangle on ungreased parchment paper. Evenly sprinkle dough with cinnamon.
4. Divide rolls between two ungreased 6-inch round nonstick baking dishes. Place one dish into air fryer basket. Adjust the temperature to 375F (190C) and set the timer for 10 minutes.
5. Cinnamon rolls will be done when golden around the edges and mostly firm. Repeat with second dish. Allow rolls to cool in dishes 10 minutes before serving.

Nutrition:

Calories: 145

Fat: 10g

Protein: 8g

Carbohydrates: 10g

Fiber: 1g

3. Cheesy Omelet

Preparation time: 5 minutes　　　**Cooking time:** 12 minutes　　　**Servings:** 2

Ingredients:

- 4 large eggs
- 1½ cups chopped fresh spinach leaves
- 2 tablespoons peeled and chopped yellow onion
- 2 tablespoons salted butter, melted
- ½ cup shredded mild Cheddar cheese
- ¼ teaspoon salt

Directions:

1. In an ungreased 6-inch round nonstick baking dish, whisk eggs. Stir in spinach, onion, butter, Cheddar, and salt.
2. Place dish into air fryer basket. Adjust the temperature to 320F (160C) and set the timer for 12 minutes. Omelet will be done when browned on the top and firm in the middle.
3. Slice in half and serve warm on two medium plates.

Nutrition:

Calories: 368

Fat: 28g

Protein: 20g

Carbohydrates: 3g

Fiber: 1g

4. Air Fried Cheese Soufflés

Preparation time: 15 minutes   **Cooking time:** 12 minutes   **Servings:** 4

Ingredients:

- 3 large eggs, whites and yolks separated
- ¼ teaspoon cream of tartar
- ½ cup shredded sharp Cheddar cheese
- 3 ounces (85 g) cream cheese, softened

Directions:

1. In a large bowl, set egg whites together with cream of tartar until soft peaks form, about 2 minutes.
2. In a medium bowl, set egg yolks, Cheddar, and cream cheese together until frothy, about 1 minute. Add egg yolk mixture to whites, gently folding until combined.
3. Pour mixture evenly into four 4-inch ramekins greased with cooking spray. Place ramekins into air fryer basket. Adjust the temperature to 350F (180C) and set the timer for 12 minutes. Eggs will be browned on the top and firm in the center when done. Serve warm.

Nutrition:

Calories: 183

Fat: 14g

Protein: 9g

Carbohydrates: 1g

Fiber: 0g

5. Bacon and Cheese Quiche

Preparation time: 5 minutes   **Cooking time:** 12 minutes   **Servings:** 2

Ingredients:

- 3 large eggs
- 2 tablespoons heavy whipping cream
- ¼ teaspoon salt
- 4 slices cooked sugar-free bacon, crumbled
- ½ cup shredded mild Cheddar cheese

Directions:

1. In a bowl, beat eggs, cream, and salt together until combined. Mix in bacon and Cheddar.
2. Pour mixture evenly into two ungreased 4-inch ramekins. Place into air fryer basket. Adjust the temperature to 320F (160C) and set the timer for 12 minutes. Quiche will be fluffy and set in the middle when done.
3. Let quiche cool in ramekins 5 minutes. Serve warm.

Nutrition:

Calories: 380

Fat: 28g

Protein: 24g

Carbohydrates: 2g

Fiber: 0g

6. Sausage Cheese Meatball

Preparation time: 10 minutes   **Cooking time:** 15 minutes   **Servings:** 18 meatballs

Ingredients:

- 1 pound (454 g) ground pork breakfast sausage
- ½ teaspoon salt
- ¼ teaspoon ground black pepper
- ½ cup shredded sharp Cheddar cheese
- 1 ounce (28 g) cream cheese, softened
- 1 large egg, whisked

Directions:

1. Combine all ingredients in a large bowl. Form mixture into eighteen 1-inch meatballs.
2. Place meatballs into ungreased air fryer basket. Set the heat to 400F and set the timer for 15 minutes, shaking basket three times during cooking. Meatballs will be browned on the outside and have an internal temperature of at least 145F (63C) when completely cooked. Serve warm.

Nutrition:

Calories: 288

Fat: 24g

Protein: 11g

Carbohydrates: 1g

Fiber: 0g

7. Sausage Burger with Avocado

Preparation time: 5 minutes   **Cooking time:** 15 minutes   **Servings:** 4

Ingredients:
- 1 pound (454 g) ground turkey breakfast sausage
- ½ teaspoon salt
- ¼ teaspoon ground black pepper
- ¼ cup seeded and chopped green bell pepper
- 2 tablespoons mayonnaise
- 1 medium avocado, peeled, pitted, and sliced

Directions:
1. In a large bowl, mix sausage with salt, black pepper, bell pepper, and mayonnaise. Form meat into four patties.
2. Place patties into ungreased air fryer basket. Set the temperature to 370F and set the timer for 15 minutes, turning patties halfway through cooking. Burgers will be done when dark brown and they have an internal temperature of at least 165F (74C).
3. Serve burgers topped with avocado slices on four medium plates.

Nutrition:
Calories: 276

Fat: 17g

Protein: 22g

Carbohydrates: 4g

Fiber: 3g

8. Bacon Cheese Pizza

Preparation time: 5 minutes   **Cooking time:** 10 minutes   **Servings:** 2

Ingredients:
- 1 cup shredded Mozzarella cheese
- 1 ounce (28 g) cream cheese, broken into small pieces
- 4 slices cooked sugar-free bacon, chopped
- ¼ cup chopped pickled jalapeños
- 1 large egg, whisked
- ¼ teaspoon salt

Directions:
1. Place Mozzarella in a single layer on the bottom of an ungreased 6-inch round nonstick baking dish. Scatter cream cheese pieces, bacon, and jalapeños over Mozzarella, then pour egg evenly around baking dish.
2. Sprinkle with salt and place into air fryer basket. Adjust the temperature to 330F (166C) and set the timer for 10 minutes. When cheese is brown and egg is set, pizza will be done.
3. Let cool on a large plate 5 minutes before serving.

Nutrition:
Calories: 361

Fat: 24g

Protein: 26g

Carbs: 5g

Fiber: 0g

9. Cheesy Pepperoni Egg

Preparation time: 5 minutes   **Cooking time:** 10 minutes   **Servings:** 2

Ingredients:
- 1 cup shredded Mozzarella cheese
- 7 slices pepperoni, chopped
- 1 large egg, whisked
- ¼ teaspoon dried oregano
- ¼ teaspoon dried parsley
- ¼ teaspoon garlic powder
- ¼ teaspoon salt

Directions:
1. Place Mozzarella in a single layer on the bottom of an ungreased 6-inch round nonstick baking dish. Scatter pepperoni over cheese, then pour egg evenly around baking dish.
2. Sprinkle with remaining ingredients and place into air fryer basket. Adjust the temperature to 330F (166C) and set the timer for 10 minutes. When cheese is brown and egg is set, dish will be done.
3. Let cool in dish 5 minutes before serving.

Nutrition:
Calories: 241

Fat: 15g

Protein: 19g

Carbohydrates: 4g

Fiber: 0g

10. Pecan Granola

Preparation time: 10 minutes   **Cooking time:** 5 minutes   **Servings:** 6

Ingredients:
- 2 cups pecans, chopped
- 1 cup unsweetened coconut flakes

- 1 cup almond slivers
- ⅓ cup sunflower seeds
- ¼ cup golden flaxseed
- ¼ cup low-carb, sugar-free chocolate chips
- ¼ cup granular Erythritol
- 2 tablespoons unsalted butter
- 1 teaspoon ground cinnamon

Directions:
1. In a large bowl, mix all ingredients.
2. Set the mixture into a 4-cup round baking dish. Place dish into the air fryer basket.
3. Adjust the temperature to 320F (160C) and set the timer for 5 minutes.
4. Allow to cool completely before serving.

Nutrition:

Calories: 617

Carbohydrates: 32g

Fat: 55g

Fiber: 11g

Protein: 11g

11. Broccoli Frittata

Preparation time: 15 minutes   **Cooking time:** 12 minutes   **Servings:** 4

Ingredients:

- 6 large eggs
- ¼ cup heavy whipping cream
- ½ cup chopped broccoli
- ¼ cup chopped yellow onion
- ¼ cup chopped green bell pepper

Directions:
1. In a bowl, whisk eggs and heavy whipping cream. Mix in broccoli, onion, and bell pepper.
2. Pour into a 6-inch round oven-safe baking dish. Set baking dish into the air fryer basket.
3. Adjust the temperature to 350F (180C) and set the timer for 12 minutes.
4. Serve warm.

Nutrition:

Calories: 168

Carbohydrates: 3g

Fat: 11g

Fiber: 1g

Protein: 10g

12. Smoky Sausage Patties

Preparation time: 10 minutes   **Cooking time:** 9 minutes   **Servings:** 8

Ingredients:

- 1 pound (454 g) ground pork
- 1 tablespoon coconut aminos
- 2 teaspoons liquid smoke
- 1 teaspoon dried sage
- 1 teaspoon sea salt
- ½ teaspoon fennel seeds
- ½ teaspoon dried thyme
- ½ teaspoon freshly ground black pepper
- ¼ teaspoon cayenne pepper

Directions:
1. In a large bowl, combine the pork, coconut aminos, liquid smoke, sage, salt, fennel seeds, thyme, black pepper, and cayenne pepper. Work the meat with your hands until the seasonings are fully incorporated.
2. Shape the mixture into 8 equal-size patties. Set the patties on a plate and cover with plastic wrap. Freeze the patties for at least 30 minutes.
3. Working in batches, if necessary, set the patties in a single layer in the air fryer, being careful not to overcrowd them.
4. Set the air fryer to 400F (204C) and air fry for 5 minutes. Bend and cook for about 4 minutes more.

Nutrition:

Calories: 204

Carbohydrates: 17g

Fat: 18g

Fiber: 2g

Protein: 6g

13. Aromatic Cake

Preparation time: 10 minutes   **Cooking time:** 7 minutes   **Servings:** 4

Ingredients:

- ½ cup finely ground almond flour
- ¼ cup Erythritol

- ½ tsp. baking powder
- 2 tbsp. unsalted butter, softened
- 1 large egg

- ½ tsp. unflavored gelatin
- ½ tsp. vanilla extract
- ½ tsp. ground cinnamon

Directions:
1. In a large bowl, merge almond flour, Erythritol, and baking powder. Attach butter, egg, gelatin, vanilla, and cinnamon. Pour into 6-inch round baking pan.
2. Place pan into the air fryer basket.
3. Adjust the temperature to 300F (150C) and set the timer for 7 minutes.
4. Cut cake into four and serve.

Nutrition:

Calories: 153

Carbohydrates: 13g

Fat: 13g

Fiber: 2g

Protein: 5g

14. Cheesy Cauliflower Hash Browns

Preparation time: 20 minutes   **Cooking time:** 12 minutes   **Servings:** 4

Ingredients:

- 1 (12 ounce / 340-g) steamer bag cauliflower
- 1 large egg

- 1 cup shredded sharp Cheddar cheese

Directions:
1. Set bag in microwave and cook according to package instructions. Allow to cool completely and set cauliflower into a cheesecloth or kitchen towel and squeeze to remove excess moisture.
2. Press cauliflower with a fork and add egg and cheese.
3. Divide a piece of parchment to fit your air fryer basket. Set ¼ of the mixture and form it into a hash brown patty shape. Set it onto the parchment and into the air fryer basket, working in batches if necessary.
4. Adjust the temperature to 400F (205C) and set the timer for 12 minutes.
5. Serve immediately.

Nutrition:

Calories: 153

Carbohydrates: 5g

Fat: 9g

Fiber: 2g

Protein: 10g

15. Cheesy Sausage Pepper

Preparation time: 15 minutes   **Cooking time:** 15 minutes   **Servings:** 4

Ingredients:

- ½ pound (227 g) spicy ground pork breakfast sausage
- 4 large eggs
- 4 ounces (113 g) full-fat cream cheese

- ¼ cup canned diced tomatoes and green chilies, drained
- 4 large poblano peppers
- 8 tablespoons shredded pepper jack cheese
- ½ cup full-fat sour cream

Directions:
1. In a skillet over medium heat, crumble and brown the ground sausage until no pink remains. Detach sausage and drain the fat from the pan. Crack eggs into the pan, scramble, and cook until no longer runny.
2. Set cooked sausage in a large bowl and fold in cream cheese. Merge in diced tomatoes and chiles. Gently fold in eggs.
3. Cut a 4-5-inch slit in the top of each poblano. Separate the filling into four servings and spoon carefully into each pepper. Set each with 2 tablespoons pepper jack cheese.
4. Set each pepper into the air fryer basket.
5. Adjust the temperature to 350F (180C) and set the timer for 15 minutes.
6. Serve immediately with sour cream on top.

Nutrition:

Calories: 489

Carbohydrates: 13g

Fat: 35g

Fiber: 4g

Protein: 23g

16. Cheesy Egg

Preparation time: 5 minutes   **Cooking time:** 15 minutes   **Servings:** 2

Ingredients:

- 4 large eggs
- 2 tablespoons unsalted butter, melted
- ½ cup shredded sharp Cheddar cheese

Directions:

1. Set eggs into 2-cup round baking dish and whisk. Set dish into the air fryer basket.
2. Adjust the temperature to 400F (205C) and set the timer for 10 minutes.
3. After 5 minutes, stir the eggs and attach the butter and cheese. Let cook 3 minutes and stir again.
4. Use a fork to fluff. Serve warm.

Nutrition:

Calories: 359   Carbohydrates: 1g

Fat: 27g   Fiber: 0g

Protein: 20g

17. Bacon Cheese Egg with Avocado

Preparation time: 15 minutes   **Cooking time:** 20 minutes   **Servings:** 4

Ingredients:

- 6 large eggs
- ¼ cup heavy whipping cream
- 1½ cups chopped cauliflower
- 1 cup shredded medium Cheddar cheese
- 1 medium avocado, peeled and pitted
- 8 tablespoons full-fat sour cream
- 2 scallions, sliced on the bias
- 12 slices sugar-free bacon, cooked and crumbled

Directions:

1. In a medium bowl, set eggs and cream together. Pour into a 4-cup round baking dish.
2. Add cauliflower and mix, and then top with Cheddar. Place dish into the air fryer basket.
3. Adjust the temperature to 320F (160C) and set the timer for 20 minutes.
4. When completely done, eggs will be firm and cheese will be browned. Slice into four pieces.
5. Di avocado and divide evenly among pieces. Set each piece with 2 tablespoons sour cream, sliced scallions, and crumbled bacon.

Nutrition:

Calories: 512   Carbohydrates: 8g

Fat: 38g   Fiber: 3g

Protein: 27g

18. Cheesy Avocado Cauliflower

Preparation time: 15 minutes   **Cooking time:** 8 minutes   **Servings:** 2

Ingredients:

- 1 (12 ounce / 340-g) steamer bag cauliflower
- 1 large egg
- ½ cup shredded Mozzarella cheese
- 1 ripe medium avocado
- ½ teaspoon garlic powder
- ¼ teaspoon ground black pepper

Directions:

1. Set cauliflower according to package instructions. Detach from bag and place into cheesecloth or clean towel to remove excess moisture.
2. St cauliflower into a large bowl and mix in egg and Mozzarella. Divide a piece of parchment to fit your air fryer. Set the cauliflower mixture into two and place it on the parchment in two mounds. Mash out the cauliflower mounds into a ¼-inch-thick rectangle. Set the parchment into the air fryer basket.
3. Adjust the temperature to 400F (20C) and set the timer for 8 minutes.
4. Bend the cauliflower halfway through the cooking time.
5. When the timer beeps, detach the parchment and allow the cauliflower to cool 5 minutes.
6. Cut open the avocado and detach the pit. Spoon out the inside, place it in a medium bowl, and mash it with garlic powder and pepper. Spread onto the cauliflower. Serve immediately.

Nutrition:

Calories: 278   Protein: 14g

Fat: 15g   Carbohydrates: 16g

Fiber: 8g

19. Air Fried Spaghetti Squash

Preparation time: 15 minutes   **Cooking time:** 8 minutes   **Servings:** 4

Ingredients:

- 2 cups cooked spaghetti squash
- 2 tbsp. unsalted butter
- 1 large egg
- ¼ cup finely ground almond flour
- 2 stalks green onion
- ½ teaspoon garlic powder
- 1 teaspoon dried parsley

Directions:

1. Detach excess moisture from the squash using a cheesecloth or kitchen towel.
2. Mix all ingredients in a large bowl. Form into four patties.
3. Divide a piece of parchment to fit your air fryer basket. Set each patty on the parchment and place into the air fryer basket.
4. Adjust the temperature to 400F (205C) and set the timer for 8 minutes.
5. Bend the patties halfway through the cooking time. Serve warm.

Nutrition:

Calories: 131

Fat: 10g

Protein: 4g

Carbohydrates: 7g

Fiber: 2g

20. Lettuce Wrap with Bacon

Preparation time: 20 minutes   **Cooking time:** 13 minutes   **Servings:** 4

Ingredients:

- 8 ounces (227 g) (about 12 slices) reduced-sodium bacon
- 8 tablespoons mayonnaise
- 8 large romaine lettuce leaves
- 4 Roma tomatoes, sliced
- Salt and freshly ground black pepper

Directions:

1. Set the bacon in a single layer in the air fryer basket. Set the air fryer to 350F (180C) and cook for 10 minutes. Check for crispiness and cook for 2 to 3 minutes longer if needed. Cook in batches, if necessary, and drain the grease in between batches.
2. Spread 1 tbsp. of mayonnaise on each of the lettuce leaves and top with the tomatoes and cooked bacon. Flavor to taste with salt and freshly ground black pepper. Roll the lettuce leaves as you would a burrito, securing with a toothpick if desired.

Nutrition:

Calories: 370

Fat: 34g

Protein: 11g

Carbohydrates: 7g

Fiber: 3g

Lunch

21. Paprika Whole Chicken

Preparation time: 15 minutes   **Cooking time:** 75 minutes   **Servings:** 12

Ingredients:

- 6 lbs. whole chicken
- 1 tsp. kosher salt
- 1 tsp. ground black pepper
- 1 tsp. ground paprika
- 1 tbsp. minced garlic
- 3 tbsp. butter
- 1 tsp. olive oil
- ¼ c. water
- 3 oz. chive stems

Directions:

1. Rub the whole chicken with kosher salt and ground black pepper inside and outside. Sprinkle it with the ground paprika and minced garlic.
2. Dice the chives. Put the diced chives inside the whole chicken.
3. Then add the butter. Rub the chicken with olive oil.
4. Preheat the Air Fryer to 360F and pour water into the Air Fryer basket.
5. Set the chicken on the rack inside the Air Fryer. Cook the chicken for 75 minutes.
6. When the chicken is cooked, it should have slightly crunchy skin.
7. Cut the cooked chicken into the servings.

Nutrition:

Calories: 464

Fat: 20.1g

Fiber: 0.2g

Carbohydrates: 0.9g

Protein: 65.8g

22. Parmesan Frittata

Preparation time: 10 minutes   **Cooking time:** 15 minutes   **Servings:** 6

Ingredients :

- 6 eggs
- ⅓ c. heavy cream
- 1 tomato
- 5 oz. chive stems
- 1 tbsp. butter
- 1 tsp. salt
- 1 tbsp. dried oregano
- 6 oz. parmesan
- 1 tsp. chili pepper

Directions:

1. Crack the eggs into the Air Fryer basket tray and whisk them with a hand whisker.
2. Chop the tomato and dice the chives.
3. Add the vegetables to the egg mixture.
4. Pour the heavy cream.
5. Sprinkle the liquid mixture with butter, salt, dried oregano, and chili pepper.
6. Shred Parmesan cheese and attach it to the mixture too.
7. Sprinkle the mixture with a silicone spatula.
8. Preheat the Air Fryer to 375F and cook the frittata for 15 minutes.

Nutrition:

Calories: 202

Fat: 15g

Fiber: 0.7g

Carbohydrates: 3.4g

Protein: 15.1g

23. Crispy Pork Bites

Preparation time: 5 minutes   **Cooking time:** 25 minutes   **Servings:** 2

Ingredients:

- 1 medium onion
- ½ pound pork belly
- ½tbsp. coconut cream
- 1 tbsp. butter
- Salt & pepper, to taste

Directions:

1. Slice the pork belly into even and thin strips

2. The onion must be diced.
3. Transfer all the ingredients into a mixing bowl and allow it to marinate in the fridge for the next two hours.
4. Fix the temperature to 350F and preheat the air-fryer for 5 minutes.
5. Keep the pork strips inside the air-fryer and let it cook for 25 minutes at a temperature of 350F.
6. Enjoy!

Nutrition:

Calories: 448

Fat: 42g

Carbohydrates: 2g

Protein: 20g

24. Asparagus with Garlic

Preparation time: 5 minutes　　**Cooking time:** 10 minutes　　**Servings:** 4

Ingredients:

- 1 pound asparagus, rinsed, ends snapped off where they naturally break
- ½ teaspoons olive oil
- 2 garlic cloves, minced
- ½ tablespoons balsamic vinegar
- ½ teaspoon dried thyme

Directions:

1. In a huge bowl, mix the asparagus with olive oil. Transfer to the air fryer basket.
2. Sprinkle with garlic. Roast for 4 to 5 minutes for crisp-tender or for 8 to 11 minutes for asparagus.
3. Drizzle with the balsamic vinegar and sprinkle with the thyme leaves. Serve immediately.

Nutrition:

Calories: 41

Fat: 1g

Protein: 3g

Carbohydrates: 6g

Sodium: 3mg

25. Creamy Kebab

Preparation time: 15 minutes　　**Cooking time:** 10 minutes　　**Servings:** 5

Ingredients:

- 14 oz. chicken fillet
- ½ cup heavy cream
- 1 teaspoon kosher salt
- ½ teaspoon ground black pepper
- 1 teaspoon turmeric
- 1 teaspoon curry powder
- 1 teaspoon olive oil

Directions:

1. Combine the heavy cream with the kosher salt, ground black pepper, turmeric, and curry powder.
2. Whisk the mixture well.
3. Add oil and whisk again.
4. Cut the chicken fillet into pieces.
5. Add the chicken to the heavy cream mixture and stir carefully.
6. Preheat the air fryer to 360F.
7. Put the chicken kebab in the air fryer rack and cook it for 10 minutes.

Nutrition:

Calories: 204

Fat: 11.4g

Fiber: 0.3g

Carbohydrates: 1g

Protein: 23.3g

26. Coconut Pancake Hash

Preparation time: 7 minutes　　**Cooking time:** 9 minutes　　**Servings:** 9

Ingredients:

- 1 teaspoon baking soda
- 1 tablespoon apple cider vinegar
- 1 teaspoon salt
- 1 teaspoon ground ginger
- 1 cup coconut flour
- 5 tablespoons butter
- 1 egg
- ¼ cup heavy cream

Directions:

1. Combine the baking soda, salt, ground ginger, and flour in a bowl.
2. Take a separate bowl and crack in the egg. Add butter and heavy cream.

3. Use a hand mixer and mix well. Combine the dry and liquid mixture together and stir it until smooth.
4. Preheat the air fryer to 400F.
5. Pour the pancake mixture into the air fryer basket tray. Cook the pancake hash for 4 minutes.
6. Scramble the pancake hash well and keep cooking for 5 minutes more.
7. Transfer to serving plates and serve hot.

Nutrition:

Calories: 148

Fat: 11.3g

Fiber: 5.3g

Carbohydrates: 8.7g

Protein: 3.7g

27. Coriander Chicken

Preparation time: 20 minutes   **Cooking time:** 16 minutes   **Servings:** 4

Ingredients:

- 1 oz. fresh coriander root
- 1 teaspoon olive oil
- ½ tablespoons minced garlic
- ¼ lemon, sliced
- ½ teaspoon salt

- 1 teaspoon ground black pepper
- ½ teaspoon chili flakes
- 1 tablespoon dried parsley
- 1 pound chicken thighs

Directions:

1. Peel the fresh coriander and grate it. Then combine the olive oil with the minced garlic, salt, ground black pepper, chili flakes, and dried parsley. Combine the mixture and sprinkle over the chicken tights.
2. Add the sliced lemon and grated coriander root. Mix the chicken thighs carefully and leave them to marinate for 10 minutes in the fridge.
3. Meanwhile, preheat the air fryer to 365F.
4. Set the chicken in the air fryer basket tray. Add all the remaining liquid from the chicken and cook for 15 minutes.
5. Serve hot.

Nutrition:

Calories: 187

Fat: 11.4g

Fiber: 1g

Carbohydrates: 3.6g

Protein: 20g

28. Spinach Beef Heart

Preparation time: 15 minutes   **Cooking time:** 20 minutes   **Servings:** 4

Ingredients:

- 1 pound beef heart
- 5 oz. chive stems
- ½ cup fresh spinach
- 1 teaspoon salt

- 1 teaspoon ground black pepper
- 2cups chicken stock
- 1 teaspoon butter

Directions:

1. Remove all the fat from the beef heart. Dice the chives.
2. Chop the fresh spinach. Combine the diced chives, fresh spinach, and butter together. Stir it.
3. Make a cut in the beef heart and fill it with the spinach-chives mixture.
4. Preheat the air fryer to 400F.
5. Pour the chicken stock into the air fryer basket tray. Sprinkle the Prepared stuffed beef heart with the salt and ground black pepper. Put the beef heart in the air fryer and cook it for 20 minutes.
6. Remove the cooked heart from the air fryer and slice it.
7. Sprinkle the slices with the remaining liquid from the air fryer.

Nutrition:

Calories: 124

Fat: 7.9g

Fiber: 0.5g

Carbohydrates: 1.2g

Protein: 14.8g

29. Cheddar Salmon Casserole

Preparation time: 20 minutes   **Cooking time:** 12 minutes   **Servings:** 8

Ingredients:

- 3 oz. cheddar cheese, shredded
- ½ cup cream
- 1 pound salmon fillet
- 1 tablespoon dried dill
- 1 teaspoon dried parsley
- 1 teaspoon salt
- 1 teaspoon ground coriander
- ½ teaspoon ground black pepper
- 2 green peppers, chopped
- 1 oz. chive stems, diced
- 3 oz. bok choy, chopped
- 1 tablespoon olive oil

Directions:
1. Coat the salmon fillet with the dried dill, dried parsley, ground coriander, and ground black pepper. Massage the salmon fillet gently and leave it for 5 minutes to marinate.
2. Meanwhile, grease the air fryer casserole tray with the olive oil. Cut the salmon fillet into the cubes. Separate the salmon cubes into 2 portions.
3. Place the first portion of salmon cubes in the casserole tray. Sprinkle the fish with the chopped bok choy, diced chives, and chopped green pepper.
4. Then place the second portion of salmon cubes over the vegetables.
5. Sprinkle the casserole with the shredded cheese and heavy cream.
6. Preheat the air fryer to 380F.
7. Cook the salmon casserole for 12 minutes (once the dish is cooked it will have a crunchy light brown crust).

Nutrition:
Calories: 124
Fat: 4.9g
Fiber: 0.5g
Carbohydrates: 1.2g
Protein: 4.8g

30. Indian Lamb Meatballs

Preparation time: 10 minutes   **Cooking time:** 14 minutes   **Servings:** 8

Ingredients:
- 1 garlic clove
- 1 tablespoon butter
- 4 oz. chive stems
- ¼ tablespoon turmeric
- ⅓ teaspoon cayenne pepper
- 1 teaspoon ground coriander
- ¼ teaspoon bay leaf
- 1 teaspoon salt
- 1 pound ground lamb
- 1 egg
- 1 teaspoon ground black pepper

Directions:
1. Peel the garlic clove and mince it Combine the minced garlic with the ground lamb.
2. Coat the meat mixture with the turmeric, cayenne pepper, ground coriander, bay leaf, salt, and ground black pepper. Crack the egg in the meat. Finely chop the chives and add them in the lamb. Mix well to combine.
3. Preheat the air fryer to 400F.
4. Put the butter in the air fryer basket tray and melt it. Make the meatballs from the lamb mixture and place them in the air fryer basket tray.
5. Cook for 14 minutes, stirring occasionally.

Nutrition:
Calories: 198
Fat: 6.8g
Fiber: 0.5g
Carbohydrates: 2.3g
Protein: 30.7g

31. Lamb Kleftiko

Preparation time: 25 minutes   **Cooking time:** 30 minutes   **Servings:** 6

Ingredients:
- 1 oz. garlic clove, peeled
- 1 tablespoon dried oregano
- ½ lemon
- ¼ tablespoon ground cinnamon
- 1 tablespoons butter, frozen
- 18 oz. leg of lamb
- 1 cup heavy cream
- 1 teaspoon bay leaf
- 1 teaspoon dried mint
- 1 tablespoon olive oil

Directions:

1. Mash the garlic cloves and combine them with the dried oregano, and ground cinnamon. Chop the lemon. Coat the leg of lamb with the crushed garlic mixture.
2. Rub it with the chopped lemon. Combine the heavy cream, bay leaf, and dried mint together.
3. Whisk the mixture well. Add the olive oil and whisk it one more time more.
4. Pour the cream mixture on the leg of lamb and stir it carefully. Leave the leg of lamb for 10 minutes to marinade.
5. Preheat the air fryer to 380 F.
6. Chop the butter and coat over the lamb.
7. Place the leg of lamb in the air fryer basket tray and coat it with the remaining cream mixture. Then add the chopped butter over the meat.
8. Cook for 30 minutes.
9. Remove the meat from the air fryer and sprinkle it gently with the remaining cream mixture. Serve hot.

Nutrition:

Calories: 131

Fat: 10g

Protein: 4g

Carbohydrates: 7g

Fiber: 2g

32. Beef Meatballs

Preparation time: 15 minutes   **Cooking time:** 11 minutes   **Servings:** 6

Ingredients:

- 1 tablespoon almond flour
- 1 pound ground beef
- 1 teaspoon dried parsley
- 1 teaspoon dried dill
- ½ teaspoon ground nutmeg
- 1 oz. chive stems
- 1 teaspoon garlic powder
- 1 teaspoon salt
- ½ cup heavy cream
- ¼ cup chicken stock
- 1 teaspoon mustard
- 1 teaspoon ground black pepper
- 1 tablespoon butter

Directions:

1. Combine the ground beef and almond flour together in the bowl.
2. Add the dried dill, dried parsley, ground nutmeg, garlic powder, chopped chives, salt, ground black pepper, and mustard.
3. Mix well to combine.
4. Make the meatballs from the mixture.
5. Preheat the air fryer to 380F.
6. Set the meatballs in the air fryer basket tray.
7. Add the butter and cook the dish for 5 minutes.
8. Turn the meatballs over.
9. Coat the meatballs with the heavy cream and chicken stock.
10. Cook for 6 minutes more.
11. Serve immediately with the cream gravy.

Nutrition:

Calories: 198

Fat: 6.8g

Fiber: 0.5g

Carbohydrates: 2.3g

Protein: 30.7g

33. Corn Chive Beef

Preparation time: 10 minutes   **Cooking time:** 19 minutes   **Servings:** 3

Ingredients:

- 1 oz. chive stems
- 1 teaspoon black pepper
- ¼ teaspoon cayenne pepper
- 1 cup water
- 1 pound minced beef
- 1 teaspoon butter
- ½ teaspoon ground paprika

Directions:

1. Dice the chives finely. Pour water into the pizza tray and place the diced chives.
2. Sprinkle the chives with the black pepper, cayenne pepper, and ground paprika.

3. Add water and mix the chives up carefully.
4. Preheat the air fryer to 400F and put the tray into the air fryer basket.
5. Cook the chives for 4 minutes. Detach the tray from the air fryer and add the minced garlic.
6. Combine the chives-meat mixture carefully and return it back in the air fryer.
7. Cook the beef mixture for 7 minutes at the same temperature. Mix the meat mixture carefully with the help of a fork and cook for 8 minutes more. Remove the cooked beef from the air fryer and mix it gently with a fork.
8. Transfer the cooked beef to serving plates.

Nutrition:

Calories: 359

Fat: 27g

Protein: 20g

Carbohydrates: 1g

Fiber: 0g

34. Chicken Goulash

Preparation time: 10 minutes   **Cooking time:** 17 minutes   **Servings:** 6

Ingredients:

- 4 oz. chive stems
- 2 green peppers, chopped
- 1 teaspoon olive oil
- 14 oz. ground chicken
- 3 tomatoes

- ½ cup chicken stock
- 1 garlic clove, sliced
- 1 teaspoon salt
- 1 teaspoon ground black pepper
- 1 teaspoon mustard

Directions:

1. Chop chives roughly.
2. Spray the air fryer basket tray with the olive oil.
3. Preheat the air fryer to 365 F.
4. Put the chopped chives in the air fryer basket tray.
5. Add the chopped green pepper and cook the vegetables for 5 minutes.
6. Add the ground chicken.
7. Chop the tomatoes into the small cubes and add them in the air fryer mixture too.
8. Cook the mixture for 6 minutes more.
9. Add the chicken stock, sliced garlic cloves, salt, ground black pepper, and mustard.
10. Mix well to combine.
11. Cook the goulash for 6 minutes more.

Nutrition:

Calories: 38

Fat: 1.7g

Fiber: 2.3g

Carbohydrates: 4.5g

Protein: 1.8g

35. Sausages with Butterbean and Tomato Ratatouille

Preparation time: 10 minutes   **Cooking time:** 45 minutes   **Servings:** 2

Ingredients:

- 4 sausages

For the Ratatouille:

- 1 chopped pepper
- 2 diced courgettis
- 1 diced aborigine
- 1 diced medium red onion
- 1 tbsp. olive oil
- 3½ cups of drained and rinsed butterbeans

- 3½ cups of chopped tomatoes
- 2 sprigs thyme
- 1 tbsp. balsamic vinegar
- 2 chopped garlic cloves
- 1 finely chopped red chili

Directions:

1. For 3 minutes, heat the Air fryer to 200C.
2. Now add the courgettis, pepper, aborigine, onion and oil and roast for approximately 20 minutes until the veg has blistered on the skin.
3. Remove and leave to cool.
4. Turn the Air fryer down to 180C.

5. Merge the veg with the rest of the ratatouille ingredients in a saucepan and bring to a simmer before seasoning.
6. Now place the sausages to the Air fryer, make sure they don't touch each other.
7. Cook for 10 to 15 minutes and shake once during the cooking time. Serve and enjoy!

Nutrition:

Calories: 198

Fat: 6.8g

Fiber: 0.5g

Carbohydrates: 2.3g

Protein: 30.7g

36. Buttermilk Chicken with Sweet Potato Chips

Preparation time: 10 minutes   **Cooking time:** 17 minutes   **Servings:** 2

Ingredients:

For the Chicken:

- 200 ml buttermilk
- ½ tsp. cayenne pepper
- 1 tsp. minced garlic
- 2 150 g chicken breasts

- 4 tbsp. plain flour seasoned with salt and pepper
- 1 egg
- 200 g panko breadcrumbs

For the Chips:

- 2 sweet potatoes, skinned and sliced into 1 cm thick chips
- 1 tbsp. olive oil

- 1 tbsp. sweet smoked paprika

Directions:

1. In a bowl, place the buttermilk, cayenne and garlic with the chicken breasts. Cover and marinate overnight in the refrigerator.
2. Heat the Air fryer for 3 minutes.
3. Rub the marinade off the chicken.
4. Then sink the breasts into a bowl of seasoned flour, then in the beaten egg and then the breadcrumbs make sure that the chicken is well coated.
5. Place the chicken in the Air fryer for 20 minutes at 190C.
6. Toss the chips in oil and paprika and place in the Air fryer.
7. Cook at 190C for 20 minutes.
8. Season the chips with salt and pepper. Serve and enjoy!

Nutrition:

Calories 200

Carbohydrates: 18g

Fat: 4g

Protein: 22g

37. Vegetable Crisps and Cheesy Pesto Twists

Preparation time: 10 minutes   **Cooking time:** 17 minutes   **Servings:** 4

Ingredients:

For the Vegetable Crisps:

- 2 parsnips
- 2 beetroots
- 1 medium sweet potato, peeled

- 1 tbsp. olive oil
- ½ tsp. chili powder

For the Cheesy Pesto Twists:

- 1 11 oz. pack of all-butter puff pastry
- 1 tbsp. almond flour
- ½ cup of cream cheese

- 4 tbsp. pesto
- 1 egg, beaten
- ½ cup of grated parmesan

Directions:

1. Heat the air fryer to 240C.
2. Slice super-thin strips off the parsnips, beetroot and sweet potato with a peeler.
3. Set the vegetable slices in the oil and chili powder, then season with salt and pepper.
4. Cook in the Air fryer until crisp and golden.
5. For the cheesy pesto twists, set the pastry into a rectangle on a lightly floured surface with its short side horizontal and the long side vertical.
6. D in half down the middle.

7. Spread cream cheese and pesto over one half and set the other piece of pastry on top to create a sandwich.
8. Divide in half down the middle again to create 2 large rectangles.
9. Slice each rectangle into 1 cm-thick horizontal strips.
10. Twist gently each pastry strip, pulling to lengthen.
11. Brush the twists lightly with beaten egg and scatter with Parmesan.
12. Now air fry for 20 to 25 minutes until risen and golden brown. Serve and enjoy!

Nutrition:
Calories: 126
Protein: 4.13g

Fat: 10.76g
Carbohydrates: 3.34g

38. Salmon with Creamy Courgetti

Preparation time: 10 minutes   **Cooking time:** 17 minutes   **Servings:** 2
Ingredients:

- 2 5 oz. salmon fillets, skin on

For the Courgetti:

- 2 large sized straight courgettis
- 1 ripe avocado
- ½ de-stoned and chopped garlic clove
- Small handful parsley, finely chopped

- 1 tsp. olive oil

- Handful cherry tomatoes
- Handful black olives
- 2 tbsp. toasted pine nuts

Directions:

1. Rub and season the salmon with oil, salt and pepper.
2. Place in the Air fryer at 180C for 10 minutes until the skin turns crisp.
3. Prepare the courgetti by using a spiralizer peeler and set to one side.
4. For the sauce, chop the avocado, parsley, garlic and add some seasoning and blend in a chopper until smooth.
5. Toss the courgetti in the blended sauce and top with the salmon.
6. Scatter the pine nuts over the dish. Serve and enjoy!

Nutrition:
Calories: 126
Protein: 4.13g

Fat: 10.76g
Carbohydrates: 3.34g

39. French toast with Yogurt and Berries

Preparation time: 10 minutes   **Cooking time:** 17 minutes   **Servings:** 4
Ingredients:

- 2 large eggs
- 1 tsp. vanilla extract
- 2 thick sourdough slices
- Bread butter for spreading

- Mixed berries
- Squeeze of honey
- Plain low fat Greek yogurt, to serve

Directions:

1. Heat the Air fryer to 180C.
2. Beat the eggs and vanilla together. Butter both sides of the bread.
3. Sink the bread in the egg mix until it absorbs the mixture.
4. Now place the bread in the fryer basket and cook for 8 minutes.
5. When ready, serve with mixed berries, honey and yogurt.

Nutrition:
Calories: 271
Fat: 12g
Fiber: 1g

Carbohydrates: 2g
Protein: 28g

40. Squash with Cumin and Chili

Preparation time: 10 minutes   **Cooking time:** 17 minutes   **Servings:** 4
Ingredients:

- 1 medium butternut squash
- 2 tsp. cumin seeds
- 1 large pinch of chili flakes
- 1 tbsp. olive oil

- 150 ml plain Greek yogurt
- 40 g pine nuts
- 1 small bunch fresh coriander chopped

Directions:
1. Remove the seeds and slice the squash.
2. Place with the spices and oiling a bowl. Season well.
3. Heat the Air fryer to 190C.
4. Set the squash in the air fryer basket and roast for 20 minutes until soft and slightly charred.
5. When ready, serve mist coriander over the squash and serve with yogurt and the nuts. Enjoy!

Nutrition:

Calories: 393

Fat: 22g

Carbohydrates: 7g

Fiber: 1g

Carbs: 4g

Protein: 39g

Dinner

41. Korean Beef Bowl

Preparation time: 15 minutes   **Cooking time:** 18 minutes   **Servings:** 4

Ingredients:

- 1 tbsp. minced garlic
- 1 tsp. ground ginger
- 4 oz. chive stems, chopped
- 2 tbsp. apple cider vinegar
- 1 tbsp. flax seeds
- 2 tsps. olive oil
- 1 lb. ground beef
- 4 tbsp. chicken stock

Directions:

1. Coat the ground beef with the apple cider vinegar and stir the meat with a spoon.
2. Add the ground ginger, minced garlic, and olive oil. Mix well.
3. Preheat the Air Fryer to 370F.
4. Put the ground beef in the Air Fryer basket tray and cook for 8 minutes.
5. Stir the ground beef carefully and sprinkle with the chopped chives, flax seeds, olive oil, and chicken stock.
6. Merge well and cook for 10 minutes more.
7. Stir and serve hot.

Nutrition:

Calories: 563   Fat: 2 g

Carbohydrates: 2g   Protein: 35g

42. Pepper Beef Stew

Preparation time: 15 minutes   **Cooking time:** 23 minutes   **Servings:** 6

Ingredients:

- 10 oz. beef short ribs
- 1 c. chicken stock
- 1 garlic clove
- 3 oz. chive stems
- 4 oz. green peas
- ¼ tsp. salt
- 1 tsp. turmeric
- 1 green pepper
- 2 tsp. butter
- ½ tsp. chili flakes
- 4 oz. kale

Directions:

1. Preheat the Air Fryer to 360F.
2. Set the butter in the Air Fryer basket tray. Attach the beef short ribs. Sprinkle the beef short ribs with salt, turmeric, and chili flakes.
3. Cook the beef short ribs for 15 minutes.
4. Meanwhile, detach the seeds from the green pepper and chop it.
5. Chop the kale and dice the chives. When the time is over, pour the chicken stock in the beef short ribs. Add the chopped green pepper and diced chives.
6. After this, mist the mixture with the green peas. Peel the garlic clove and add it to the mixture too. Merge it up using the wooden spatula.
7. Then add the chopped kale to the stew mixture. Stir the stew mixture one more time and cook it at 360F for 8 minutes more. When the stew is cooked, let it rest a little.
8. Then merge the stew up and transfer to the serving plates.

Nutrition:

Calories: 35   Fat: 3g

Carbohydrates: 8g   Protein: 1g

43. Rosemary Basil Mushrooms

Preparation time: 10 minutes   **Cooking time:** 14 minutes   **Servings:** 4

Ingredients:

- 1 lb. mushrooms
- ½ tbsp. vinegar
- ½ tsp. ground coriander
- 1 tsp. rosemary, chopped
- 1 tbsp. basil, minced
- 1 garlic clove, minced
- Pepper and Salt

Directions:
1. Add all ingredients into the large bowl and toss well.
2. Select "Air Fry" mode.
3. Set time to 14 minutes and temperature to 350F, then press "Start."
4. The Air Fryer display will prompt you to add food once the temperature is reached, then add mushrooms into the Air Fryer basket.
5. Serve and enjoy!

Nutrition:

Calories: 256

Carbohydrates: 8g

Fat: 21g

Protein: 16g

44. Brine Soaked Turkey

Preparation time: 10 minutes   **Cooking time:** 45 minutes   **Servings:** 8

Ingredients:
- 7 lb. bone-in, skin-on turkey breast

Brine:
- ½ cup salt
- 1 lemon
- ½ onion
- 3 cloves garlic, smashed

- 5 sprigs fresh thyme
- 3 bay leaves
- Black pepper

Turkey Breast:
- 4 tablespoons of butter, softened
- ½ teaspoon black pepper
- ½ teaspoon garlic powder

- ¼ teaspoon dried thyme
- ¼ teaspoon dried oregano

Directions:
1. Mix the turkey brine ingredients in a pot and soak the turkey in the brine overnight. Next day, remove the soaked turkey from the brine.
2. Whisk the butter, black pepper, garlic powder, oregano, and thyme. Brush the butter mixture over the turkey then places it in a baking tray.
3. Press "Power Button" of Air Fry Oven and turn the dial to select the "Air Roast" mode. Press the Time button and again turn the dial to set the cooking time to 45 minutes
4. Now push the Temp button and rotate the dial to set the temperature at 370F. Once preheated, place the turkey baking tray in the oven and close its lid.
5. Slice and serve warm.

Nutrition:

Calories: 25

Carbohydrates: 0.2g

Fat: 2g

Protein: 0.1g

45. Crunchy Fish Sticks

Preparation time: 10 minutes   **Cooking time:** 15 minutes   **Servings:** 5

Ingredients:
- 12 oz. tilapia loins, cut into fish sticks
- ½ cup parmesan cheese, grated 3.5
- oz. pork rind, crushed

- 1 teaspoon paprika
- 1 teaspoon garlic powder
- ¼ cup mayonnaise

Directions:
1. In a shallow bowl, mix parmesan cheese, crushed pork rind, paprika, and garlic powder.
2. Add fish pieces and mayonnaise into the mixing bowl and mix well.
3. Place the cooking tray in the air fryer basket.
4. Select Air Fry mode.
5. Set time to 15 minutes and temperature 380F then press START.
6. The air fryer display will prompt you to ADD FOOD once the temperature is reached then coat fish pieces with parmesan mixture and place in the air fryer basket.
7. Serve and enjoy.

Nutrition:

Calories: 200

Carbohydrates: 1.5g

Fat: 1.3g

Protein: 0.5g

46. Stuffed Jalapeño

Preparation time: 10 minutes   **Cooking time:** 10 minutes   **Servings:** 4

Ingredients:

- 1 lb. ground pork sausage
- 1 (8 oz.) package cream cheese, softened
- 1 c. shredded Parmesan cheese
- 1 lb. large fresh jalapeño peppers, halved lengthwise and seeded
- 1 (8 oz.) bottle Ranch dressing

Directions:

1. Mix pork sausage ground with ranch dressing and cream cheese in a bowl.
2. Cut the jalapeño in half and remove their seeds.
3. Divide the cream cheese mixture into the jalapeño halves.
4. Place the jalapeño pepper in a baking tray.
5. Set the baking tray inside the Air Fryer toaster oven and close the lid.
6. Select the "Bake" mode at 350F temperature for 10 minutes.
7. Serve warm with Parmesan cheese on top.

Nutrition:

Calories: 168

Protein: 9.4g

Carbohydrates: 2.1g

Fat: 21.2g

47. Meat Bake

Preparation time: 5 minutes   **Cooking time:** 30 minutes   **Servings:** 4

Ingredients:

- 1 pound lean beef, cubed
- 1 pound pork stew meat, cubed
- 1 tablespoon spring onions, chopped
- 2 tablespoons tomato sauce
- A drizzle of olive oil
- A pinch of salt and black pepper
- ¼ teaspoon sweet paprika

Directions:

1. Heat up a pan that fits the air fryer with the oil over medium-high heat, add the pork and beef meat and brown for 5 minutes. Add the remaining ingredients, toss, introduce the pan in the air fryer and cook at 390 degrees F for 25 minutes.
2. Divide the mix between plates and serve for lunch with a side salad.

Nutrition:

Calories: 81

Protein: 0.4g

Carbohydrates: 4.7g

Fat: 8.3g

48. Chives Meatballs

Preparation time: 5 minutes   **Cooking time:** 20 minutes   **Servings:** 6

Ingredients:

- 2pound beef meat, ground
- 1 teaspoon onion powder
- 1 teaspoon garlic powder
- A pinch of salt and black pepper
- 2 tablespoons chives, chopped
- Cooking spray

Directions:

1. In a bowl, merge all the ingredients except the cooking spray, stir well and shape medium meatballs out of this mix. Pace them in your lined air fryer's basket, grease with cooking spray and cook at 360 F for 20 minutes. Serve.

Nutrition:

Calories: 120

Fat: 3.9g

Carbohydrates: 1.9g

Protein: 1.9g

49. Duo-Cheese Hake

Preparation time: 30 minutes   **Cooking time:** 17 minutes   **Servings:** 4

Ingredients:

- 1 tablespoon avocado oil
- 1 pound (454 g) hake fillets
- 1 teaspoon garlic powder
- Sea salt and ground white pepper
- 2 tablespoons shallots, chopped
- 1 bell pepper, seeded and chopped

- ½ cup Cottage cheese
- ½ cup sour cream
- 1 egg, well whisked
- 1 teaspoon yellow mustard
- 1 tablespoon lime juice
- ½ cup Swiss cheese, shredded

Directions:

1. Garnish the bottom and sides of a casserole dish with avocado oil. Add the hake fillets to the casserole dish and sprinkle with garlic powder, salt, and pepper.
2. Add the chopped shallots and bell peppers.
3. In a mixing bowl, thoroughly me the Cottage cheese, sour cream, egg, mustard, and lime juice. Pour the mixture over fish and spread evenly.
4. Cook in the preheated Air Fryer at 370F (188C) for 10 minutes.
5. Top with the Swiss cheese and cook an additional 7 minutes. Let it rest before slicing and serving. Bon appétit!

Nutrition:

Calories: 92   Carbohydrates: 13.9g

Fat: 2.1g   Protein: 5.9g

50. Almond Pickles

Preparation time: 10 minutes   **Cooking time:** 10 minutes   **Servings:** 7

Ingredients:

- 12 oz. pickles
- 2 eggs
- 1 tsp. salt

- 1 tsp. ground black pepper
- ½ cup almond flour
- 1 tbsp. olive oil

Directions:

1. Slice the pickles. Crack the eggs and whisk. Combine the salt and ground black pepper. Stir the mixture. Put the sliced pickles in the whisked egg mixture.
2. Sprinkle the sliced pickles with the salt mixture. Dip the pickles into the egg mixture again. Coat the pickles in almond flour.
3. Preheat the Air Fryer to 400F.
4. Grease the Air Fryer with olive oil. Place the sliced pickles inside and cook for 10 minutes.
5. Serve warm.

Nutrition:

Calories: 53   Carbohydrates: 1.8g

Fat: 4.4g   Protein: 2.2g

Fiber: 0.9g

51. Catfish Bites

Preparation time: 12 minutes   **Cooking time:** 16 minutes   **Servings:** 6

Ingredients:

- 1 lb. catfish fillet
- 1 tsp. minced garlic
- 2 oz. chive stems, diced
- 1 tbsp. butter, melted
- 1 tsp. turmeric

- 1 tsp. ground thyme
- 1 tsp. ground coriander
- ¼ tsp. ground nutmeg
- 1 tsp. flax seeds

Directions:

1. Cut the catfish fillet into 6 pieces.
2. Sprinkle the fish with minced garlic. Stir.
3. Add diced chives, turmeric, ground thyme, ground coriander, ground nutmeg, and flax seeds.
4. Mix the catfish bites gently.

5. Preheat the Air Fryer to 360F.
6. Coat the catfish bites with the melted butter then freeze them.
7. Put the catfish bites in the Air Fryer basket.
8. Cook the catfish bites for 16 minutes.

Nutrition:

Calories: 140

Fat: 8.7g

Fiber: 0.5g

Carbohydrates: 1.6g

Protein: 13.1g

52. Cheddar Artichoke Dip

Preparation time: 15 minutes   **Cooking time:** 27 minutes   **Servings:** 7

Ingredients:

- 1 cup spinach
- 8 oz. artichoke, chopped
- ½ cup heavy cream
- 5 oz. cheddar cheese
- ¼ tsp. salt
- 1 tsp. paprika
- ½ tsp. ground coriander
- ½ cup cream cheese
- ½ tsp. garlic powder
- 1 tsp. olive oil

Directions:

1. Put the chopped artichoke in foil. Sprinkle with salt, paprika, garlic powder, and ground coriander. Drizzle the artichokes with olive oil. Wrap the artichoke in foil.
2. Preheat the Air Fryer to 360F.
3. Place the wrapped artichoke in the Air Fryer and cook it for 25 minutes.
4. Meanwhile, chop the spinach roughly and place it in a blender. Add the heavy cream, salt, paprika, ground coriander, and cream cheese. Blend until well combined.
5. Remove the artichoke from the Air Fryer and add to the spinach mixture. Blend for 2 minutes. Pour the blended mixture into the Air Fryer. Add heavy cream.
6. Shred Cheddar cheese and add it to the Air Fryer. Stir and cook for 3 minutes at 360F.
7. When the cheese is melted, the dip is cooked.
8. Serve warm.

Nutrition:

Calories: 192

Fat: 16.4g

Fiber: 2g

Carbohydrates: 4.8g

Protein: 7.7g

53. Cilantro Tomatoes

Preparation time: 8 minutes   **Cooking time:** 12 minutes   **Servings:** 2

Ingredients:

- 2 tomatoes
- ½ tsp. salt
- 1 tsp. ground white pepper
- ½ tsp. thyme
- ½ tsp. ground coriander
- ½ tsp. cilantro
- ½ tsp. dried oregano
- 1 tbsp. olive oil

Directions:

1. Cut the tomatoes into halves.
2. Remove the flesh from the tomatoes.
3. Sprinkle the tomato halves with salt, ground white pepper, thyme, ground coriander, cilantro, and dried oregano.
4. Preheat the Air Fryer to 350F.
5. Spray the tomato halves with olive oil.
6. Place them in the Air Fryer rack.
7. Cook the tomatoes for 12 minutes.
8. When the tomatoes are done, let them cool before serving.

Nutrition:

Calories: 87

Fat: 7.3g

Fiber: 2g

Carbohydrates: 5.9g

Protein: 1.3g

54. Cinnamon Pumpkin Fries

Preparation time: 15 minutes   **Cooking time:** 15 minutes   **Servings:** 7

Ingredients:

- 1 lb. pumpkin
- 1 tsp. ground cinnamon
- ½ tsp. ground ginger
- ½ tsp. salt
- 1 tsp. olive oil
- 1 tsp. turmeric

Directions:

1. Peel the pumpkin and cut it into thick strips.
2. Coat the pumpkin strips with the ground cinnamon, ground ginger, salt, and turmeric.
3. Stir the pumpkin carefully and leave for 5 minutes to marinate.
4. Preheat the Air Fryer to 360F.
5. Drizzle the pumpkin with olive oil and transfer it to the Air Fryer basket.
6. Cook the pumpkin fries for 15 minutes, stirring occasionally.
7. Place the cooked pumpkin fries on a paper towel.
8. Chill them for 3-4 minutes before serving.

Nutrition:

Calories: 30   Carbohydrates: 5.8g
Fat: 0.8g   Protein: 0.8 g
Fiber: 2.2g

55. Winter Squash and Pumpkin Tots

Preparation time: 15 minutes   **Cooking time:** 10 minutes   **Servings:** 7

Ingredients:

- 1 cup pumpkin puree
- 1 tbsp. almond flour
- ½ tsp. ground nutmeg
- ¼ tsp. salt
- ¼ cup coconut flour
- 1 tsp. olive oil
- ¼ tsp. turmeric

Directions:

1. Take a large bowl and merge pumpkin puree, almond flour, ground nutmeg, salt, and turmeric.
2. Mix using a fork.
3. Add coconut flour.
4. Mix again. The pumpkin mixture should be non-sticky.
5. Separate the pumpkin dough into 5 and form 5 tots.
6. Preheat the Air Fryer to 360F.
7. Grease the Air Fryer with olive oil and cook the pumpkin tots for 10 minutes.

Nutrition:

Calories: 62   Carbohydrates: 7.3g
Fat: 3.6g   Protein: 1.9g
Fiber: 3.5g

56. Bacon Shrimps

Preparation time: 10 minutes   **Cooking time:** 10 minutes   **Servings:** 4

Ingredients:

- 8 oz. shrimp
- 5 oz. bacon, sliced
- 1 tsp. fresh lemon juice
- ¼ tsp. salt
- ¼ tsp. turmeric
- ½ tbsp. olive oil
- ½ tsp. dried rosemary

Directions:

1. Peel the shrimps and coat them with fresh lemon juice and salt.
2. Mix using your hands.
3. Sprinkle the shrimp with turmeric and dried rosemary.
4. Wrap the shrimp in sliced bacon.
5. Secure with toothpicks.
6. Preheat the Air Fryer to 360F.

7. Grease the Air Fryer with olive oil.
8. Put the shrimps in the Air Fryer and cook them for 5 minutes on each side.

Nutrition:

Calories: 276

Fat: 17.6g

Fiber: 0.1g

Carbohydrates: 1.6g

Protein: 26.1g

57. Almond Onion Squares

Preparation time: 15 minutes   **Cooking time:** 8 minutes   **Servings:** 8

Ingredients:

- 2 white onions
- 1 cup almond flour
- 1 tsp. baking powder
- ¼ tbsp. salt
- 1 cup heavy cream
- 1 tsp. paprika
- 1 tsp. sesame oil

Directions:

1. Set the onions and cut them into medium squares.
2. Combine the almond flour, baking powder, salt, and paprika in a large bowl.
3. Stir the dried mixture with a fork.
4. Put the onion squares in the heavy cream and coat well.
5. Sprinkle the onion squares with the dried spice mixture on each side.
6. Drizzle the onion squares with sesame oil.
7. Preheat the Air Fryer to 360F.
8. Put the onion squares in the Air Fryer and cook for 8 minutes.

Nutrition:

Calories: 89

Fat: 7.9g

Fiber: 1.1g

Carbohydrates: 4.2g

Protein: 1.4g

58. Parmesan Beans

Preparation time: 12 minutes   **Cooking time:** 5 minutes   **Servings:** 7

Ingredients:

- 14 oz. green beans
- 5 oz. parmesan, shredded
- 1 egg
- 2 tbsp. coconut flakes
- 1 tsp. dried oregano
- ½ tsp. ground paprika
- 1 tsp. butter

Directions:

1. Wash the green beans.
2. Set the egg in a bowl and whisk it.
3. Preheat the Air Fryer to 400F.
4. Place the green beans in the whisked egg.
5. Sprinkle the green beans with coconut flakes, dried oregano, and ground paprika.
6. Then add the shredded cheese and stir carefully.
7. Put the butter in the Air Fryer basket and melt it.
8. Add the green beans.
9. Cook for 5 minutes.
10. Stir the green beans and separate them into 7 servings.

Nutrition:

Calories: 103

Fat: 6.1g

Fiber: 2.2g

Carbohydrates: 5.3g

Protein: 8.4g

59. Cod Fries

Preparation time: 10 minutes   **Cooking time:** 6 minutes   **Servings:** 6

Ingredients:

- 1 lb. cod fillet
- 2 large eggs
- 1 tbsp. coconut oil
- ½ tsp. salt
- 1 tsp. ground black pepper
- 1 tsp. turmeric
- 1 tsp. paprika

Directions:

1. Cut the cod fillet into 6 parts (fries' size).
2. Set the eggs in a bowl and whisk it.
3. Add the salt, ground black pepper, turmeric, and paprika. Stir.
4. Sink the cod fillets in the egg mixture.
5. Preheat the Air Fryer to 360F.
6. Top the cod fillets with coconut oil and put them in the Air Fryer rack.
7. Cook the dish for 6 minutes, stirring after 4 minutes.
8. Remove the cooked fish fries from the Air Fryer.
9. Serve the dish with sauce.

Nutrition:

Calories: 107   Carbohydrates: 0.8g
Fat: 4.7g   Protein: 15.7g
Fiber: 0.3g

60. Mongolian Beef

Preparation time: 10 minutes   **Cooking time:** 6 minutes   **Servings:** 6

Ingredients:

- 16 oz. flank steak
- 3 tbsp. coconut flour
- 1 tbsp. olive oil
- 1 tbsp. coconut oil
- 1 tsp. ginger, grated
- 1 tbsp. garlic, chopped
- ½ tsp. salt
- 1 onion, chopped
- 1 tbsp. sesame seeds

Directions:

1. Chop the steak into the cubes and sprinkle with the coconut flour and grated ginger.
2. Add garlic and salt. Stir the mixture.
3. Pour the olive oil into the air fryer basket and preheat it at 400 F for 20 seconds.
4. Then place the chopped meat in the air fryer basket.
5. Add sesame seeds and coconut oil.
6. Stir well and cook for 10 minutes at 400F. Stir the meat every 2 minutes.
7. When the meat is cooked, remove it from the air fryer basket. Serve immediately. Enjoy!

Nutrition:

Calories: 103   Carbohydrates: 5.3g
Fat: 6.1g   Protein: 8.4g
Fiber: 2.2g

Pork, Beef and Lamb

61. Peppercorn-Crusted Beef Tenderloin

Preparation time: 10 minutes   **Cooking time:** 25 minutes   **Servings:** 6

Ingredients:

- 2 tablespoons salted butter, melted
- 2 teaspoons minced roasted garlic
- 3 tablespoons ground 4-peppercorn blend
- 1 (2-pound / 907-g) beef tenderloin, trimmed of visible fat

Directions:

1. In a small bowl, merge the butter and roasted garlic. Brush it over the beef tenderloin.
2. Put the ground peppercorns onto a plate and roll the tenderloin through them, creating a crust. Place tenderloin into the air fryer basket.
3. Adjust the temperature to 400F (204C) and roast for 25 minutes.
4. Let the tenderloin halfway through the cooking time.
5. Allow meat to rest before slicing.

Nutrition:

Calories: 289   Carbohydrates: 3g
Fat: 14g   Fiber: 1g
Protein: 35g

62. Ground Beef Taco Rolls

Preparation time: 20 minutes   **Cooking time:** 10 minutes   **Servings:** 4

Ingredients:

- ½ pound (227 g) 80/20 ground beef
- ⅓ cup water
- 1 tablespoon chili powder
- 2 teaspoons cumin
- ½ teaspoon garlic powder
- ¼ teaspoon dried oregano
- ¼ cup canned diced tomatoes and chiles, drained
- 2 tablespoons chopped cilantro
- 1½ cups Mozzarella cheese
- ½ cup finely ground almond flour
- 2 ounces (57 g) full-fat cream cheese
- 1 large egg

Directions:

1. In a skillet over medium heat, set to brown the ground beef about 7 to 10 minutes. When meat is fully cooked, drain.
2. Attach water to skillet and stir in chili powder, cumin, garlic powder, oregano, and tomatoes with chiles. Attach cilantro. Set to a boil, then reduce heat to simmer for 3 minutes.
3. In a large microwave-safe bowl, place Mozzarella, almond flour, cream cheese, and egg. Microwave for 1 minute. Set the mixture quickly until smooth ball of dough forms.
4. Divide a piece of parchment for your work surface. Set the dough into a large rectangle on the parchment, wetting your hands to prevent the dough from sticking as necessary. Divide the dough into eight rectangles.
5. On each rectangle set a few spoons of the meat mixture. Bend the short ends of each roll toward the center and roll the length as you would a burrito.
6. Divide a piece of parchment to fit your air fryer basket. Set taco rolls onto the parchment and place into the air fryer basket.
7. Adjust the temperature to 360F (182C) and air fry for 10 minutes.
8. Flip halfway through the cooking time.
9. Allow to cool 10 minutes before serving.

Nutrition:

Calories: 38   Carbohydrates: 7g
Fat: 26g   Fiber: 2g
Protein: 25g

63. Beefy Poppers

Preparation time: 15 minutes   **Cooking time:** 15 minutes   **Servings:** 8

Ingredients:

- 8 medium jalapeño peppers, stemmed, halved, and seeded
- 1 (8 ounce / 227-g) package cream cheese (or Kite Hill brand cream cheese style spread for dairy-free), softened
- 2 pounds (907 g) ground beef (85% lean)
- 1 teaspoon fine sea salt
- ½ teaspoon ground black pepper
- 8 slices thin-cut bacon
- Fresh cilantro leaves, for garnish

Directions:

1. Set the air fryer basket with avocado oil. Preheat the air fryer to 400F (204C).
2. Stuff each jalapeño half with a few tablespoons of cream cheese. Place the halves back together again to form 8 jalapeños.
3. Season the ground beef with the salt and pepper and mix with your hands to incorporate. Flatten about ¼ pound (113 g) of ground beef in the palm of your hand and place a stuffed jalapeño in the center. Fold the beef around the jalapeño, forming an egg shape. Wrap the beef-covered jalapeño with a slice of bacon and secure it with a toothpick.
4. Place the jalapeños in the air fryer basket, leaving space between them, and air fry for 15 minutes until the beef is cooked through and the bacon is crispy. Garnish with cilantro before serving.

Nutrition:

Calories: 679   Carbohydrates: 3g
Fat: 53g   Fiber: 1g
Protein: 42g

64. Swedish Meatloaf

Preparation time: 10 minutes   **Cooking time:** 35 minutes   **Servings:** 8

Ingredients:

- 1½ pounds (680 g) ground beef (85% lean)
- ¼ pound (113 g) ground pork
- 1 large egg (omit for egg-free)
- ½ cup minced onions
- ¼ cup tomato sauce

Sauce:

- ½ cup (1 stick) unsalted butter
- ½ cup shredded Swiss or mild Cheddar cheese (about 2 ounces / 57 g)
- 2 ounces (57 g) cream cheese (¼ cup), softened

- 2 tablespoons dry mustard
- 2 cloves garlic, minced
- 2 teaspoons fine sea salt
- 1 tsp. ground black pepper, plus more for garnish

- ⅓ cup beef broth
- ⅛ teaspoon ground nutmeg
- Halved cherry tomatoes, for serving (optional)

Directions:

1. Preheat the air fryer to 390F (199C).
2. In a large bowl, merge the ground beef, ground pork, egg, onions, tomato sauce, dry mustard, garlic, salt, and pepper. Using your hands, mix until well combined.
3. Set the meatloaf mixture in a loaf pan and place it in the air fryer. Bake for 35 minutes, or until cooked through and the internal temperature reaches 145°F (63°C). Check the meatloaf after 25 minutes; if it's getting too brown on the top, cover it loosely with foil to prevent burning.
4. While the meatloaf cooks, make the sauce: Heat the butter in a saucepan over medium-high heat until it sizzles and brown flecks appear, stirring constantly to keep the butter from burning. Set the heat down to low and whisk in the Swiss cheese, cream cheese, broth, and nutmeg. Simmer for at least 10 minutes.
5. When the meatloaf is done, transfer it to a serving tray and pour the sauce over it. Garnish with ground black pepper and serve with cherry tomatoes, if desired. Allow the meatloaf to rest for 10 minutes before slicing so it doesn't crumble apart.

Nutrition:

Calories: 395   Protein: 23g   Fiber: 1g
Fat: 32g   Carbohydrates: 3g

65. Salisbury steak with Mushroom Onion Gravy

Preparation time: 10 minutes   **Cooking time:** 33 minutes   **Servings:** 2

Ingredients:

Mushroom Onion Gravy:

- ¾ cup sliced button mushrooms
- ¼ cup thinly sliced onions
- ¼ cup unsalted butter, melted (or bacon fat for dairy-free)
- ½ teaspoon fine sea salt
- ¼ cup beef broth

Steaks:

- ½ pound (227 g) ground beef (85% lean)
- ¼ cup minced onions, or ½ teaspoon onion powder
- 2 tablespoons tomato paste
- 1 tablespoon dry mustard
- 1 clove garlic
- ½ teaspoon fine sea salt
- ¼ tsp. ground black pepper
- Chopped fresh thyme leaves, for garnish (optional)

Directions:

1. Preheat the air fryer to 390F (199C).
2. Make the gravy: Place the mushrooms and onions in a casserole dish that will fit in your air fryer. Set the melted butter over them and stir to coat, then season with the salt. Set the dish in the air fryer and bake for 5 minutes, stir, then cook until the onions are soft and the mushrooms are browning. Add the broth and cook for another 10 minutes.
3. While the gravy is cooking, prepare the steaks: In a large bowl, mix the ground beef, onions, tomato paste, dry mustard, garlic, salt, and pepper until well combined. Form the mixture into 2 oval-shaped patties.
4. Set the patties on top of the mushroom gravy. Air fry for 10 minutes, gently flip the patties, then cook until the beef is cooked through and the internal temperature reaches 145F (63C).
5. Transfer the steaks to a serving platter and pour the gravy over them. Garnish with ground black pepper and chopped fresh thyme, if desired.

Nutrition:

Calories: 588

Fat: 44g

Protein: 33g

Carbohydrates: 11g

Fiber: 3g

66. Fajita Meatball Lettuce Wraps

Preparation time: 10 minutes   **Cooking time:** 10 minutes   **Servings:** 4

Ingredients:

- 1 pound (454 g) ground beef (85% lean)
- ½ cup salsa, plus more for serving if desired
- ¼ cup chopped onions
- ¼ cup diced green or red bell peppers
- 1 large egg, beaten
- 1 teaspoon fine sea salt
- ½ teaspoon chili powder
- ½ teaspoon ground cumin
- 1 clove garlic, minced

For Serving (Optional):

- 8 leaves Boston lettuce
- Pico de Gallo or salsa
- Lime slices

Directions:

1. Set the air fryer basket with avocado oil. Preheat the air fryer to 350F (177C).
2. In a large bowl, mix all the ingredients until well combined.
3. Shape the meat mixture into eight 1-inch balls. Place the meatballs in the air fryer basket, leaving a little space between them. Air fry for 10 minutes, or until cooked through and no longer pink inside and the internal temperature reaches 145F (63C).
4. Serve each meatball on a lettuce leaf, topped with Pico de Gallo or salsa, if desired. Serve with lime slices if desired.

Nutrition:

Calories: 272

Fat: 18g

Protein: 23g

Carbohydrates: 3g

Fiber: 1g

67. Greek Stuffed Tenderloin

Preparation time: 10 minutes   **Cooking time:** 10 minutes   **Servings:** 4

Ingredients:

- 1½ pounds (680 g) venison or beef tenderloin, pounded to ¼ inch thick
- 3 teaspoons fine sea salt
- 1 teaspoon ground black pepper
- 2 ounces (57 g) creamy goat cheese
- ½ cup crumbled feta cheese
- ¼ cup finely chopped onions
- 2 cloves garlic, minced

For Garnish/Serving (Optional):

- Prepared yellow mustard
- Halved cherry tomatoes
- Extra-virgin olive oil
- Sprigs of fresh rosemary
- Lavender flowers

Directions:

1. Set the air fryer basket with avocado oil. Preheat the air fryer to 400F (204C).
2. Season the tenderloin on all sides with the salt and pepper.
3. In a medium-sized mixing bowl, merge the goat cheese, feta, onions, and garlic. Place the mixture in the center of the tenderloin. Tightly roll the tenderloin like a jelly roll. Tie the rolled tenderloin tightly with kitchen twine.
4. Set the meat in the air fryer basket and air fry for 5 minutes. Flip the meat over and cook for another 5 minutes, or until the internal temperature reaches 135F (57C) for medium-rare.
5. To serve, smear a line of prepared yellow mustard on a platter, then place the meat next to it and add halved cherry tomatoes on the side, if desired. Drizzle with olive oil and garnish with rosemary sprigs and lavender flowers, if desired.
6. Best served fresh.

Nutrition:

Calories: 415

Fat: 16g

Protein: 62g

Carbohydrates: 4g

Fiber: 1g

68. Herb-Crusted Lamb Chops

Preparation time: 10 minutes   **Cooking time:** 5 minutes   **Servings:** 2

Ingredients:

- 1 large egg
- 2 cloves garlic, minced
- ¼ cup pork dust
- ¼ cup powdered Parmesan cheese
- 1 tablespoon chopped fresh oregano leaves
- 1 tablespoon chopped fresh rosemary leaves
- 1 teaspoon chopped fresh thyme leaves
- ½ teaspoon ground black pepper
- 4 (1-inch-thick) lamb chops

For Garnish/Serving (Optional):

- Sprigs of fresh oregano
- Sprigs of fresh rosemary
- Sprigs of fresh thyme
- Lavender flowers
- Lemon slices

Directions:

1. Set the air fryer basket with avocado oil. Preheat the air fryer to 400F (204C).
2. Beat the egg in a shallow bowl, add the garlic, and stir well to combine. In another shallow bowl, mix the pork dust, Parmesan, herbs, and pepper.
3. One at a time, dip the lamb chops into the egg mixture, shake off the excess egg, and then dredge them in the Parmesan mixture. Use your hands to coat the chops well in the Parmesan mixture and form a nice crust on all sides; if necessary, dip the chops again in both the egg and the Parmesan mixture.
4. Set the lamb chops in the air fryer basket, leaving space between them, and air fry for 5 minutes, or until the internal temperature reaches 145F (63C) for medium doneness. Allow to rest for 10 minutes before serving.
5. Garnish with sprigs of oregano, rosemary, and thyme, and lavender flowers, if desired. Serve with lemon slices, if desired.
6. Best served fresh

Nutrition:

Calories: 790

Fat: 60g

Protein: 57g

Carbohydrates: 2g

Fiber: 1g

69. Mojito Lamb Chops

Preparation time: 5 minutes   **Cooking time:** 5 minutes   **Servings:** 2

Ingredients:

Marinade:

- 2 teaspoons grated lime zest
- ½ cup lime juice
- ¼ cup avocado oil
- ¼ cup chopped fresh mint leaves
- 4 cloves garlic, roughly chopped
- 2 teaspoons fine sea salt
- ½ teaspoon ground black pepper
- 4 (1-inch-thick) lamb chops
- Sprigs of fresh mint, for garnish (optional)
- Lime slices, for serving (optional)

Directions:

1. Make the marinade: Set all the ingredients for the marinade in a food processor or blender and purée until mostly smooth with a few small chunks. Transfer half of the marinade to a shallow dish and set the other half aside for serving. Add the lamb to the shallow dish, cover, and place in the refrigerator to marinate for at least 2 hours or overnight.
2. Set the air fryer basket with avocado oil. Preheat the air fryer to 390F (199C).
3. Remove the chops from the marinade and place them in the air fryer basket. Air fry until the internal temperature reaches 145F (63C) for medium doneness.
4. Allow the chops to rest before serving with the rest of the marinade as a sauce. Brush with fresh mint leaves and serve with lime slices, if desired. Best served fresh.

Nutrition:

Calories: 692

Fat: 53g

Protein: 48g

Carbohydrates: 5g

Fiber: 1g

70. Deconstructed Chicago Dogs

Preparation time: 10 minutes   **Cooking time:** 7 minutes   **Servings:** 4

Ingredients:

- 4 hot dogs
- 2 large dill pickles
- ¼ cup diced onions

For Garnish (Optional):

- Brown mustard
- Celery salt
- 1 tomato, cut into ½-inch dice
- 4 pickled sport peppers, diced

- Poppy seeds

Directions:

1. Set the air fryer basket with avocado oil. Preheat the air fryer to 400F (204C).
2. Place the hot dogs in the air fryer basket and air fry for 5 to 7 minutes, until hot and slightly crispy.
3. While the hot dogs cook, quarter one of the dill pickles lengthwise, so that you have 4 pickle spears. Finely dice the other pickle.
4. When the hot dogs are done, transfer them to a serving platter and arrange them in a row, alternating with the pickle spears. Top with the diced pickles, onions, tomato, and sport peppers. Drizzle brown mustard on top and garnish with celery salt and poppy seeds, if desired.
5. Best served fresh. Store leftover hot dogs in an airtight container in the refrigerator for up to 3 days. Reheat in a preheated 390F (199C) air fryer for 2 minutes, or until warmed through.

Nutrition:

Calories: 123

Fat: 8g

Protein: 8g

Carbohydrates: 3g

Fiber: 1g

71. Pork Milanese

Preparation time: 10 minutes   **Cooking time:** 12 minutes   **Servings:** 4

Ingredients:

- 4 (1-inch) boneless pork chops
- Fine sea salt and ground black pepper
- 2 large eggs
- ¾ cup powdered Parmesan cheese
- Chopped fresh parsley, for garnish
- Lemon slices, for serving

Directions:

1. Set the air fryer basket with avocado oil. Preheat the air fryer to 400F (204C).
2. Set the pork chops between 2 sheets of plastic wrap and pound them with the flat side of a meat tenderizer. Lightly season both sides of the chops with salt and pepper.
3. Lightly beat the eggs in a bowl. Divide the Parmesan cheese evenly between 2 bowls and set the bowls in this order: Parmesan, eggs, Parmesan. Dredge a chop in the first bowl of Parmesan, then dip it in the eggs, and then set it again in the second bowl of Parmesan, making sure both sides and all edges are well coated. Repeat with the remaining chops.
4. Put the chops in the air fryer basket and air fry for 12 minutes, or until the internal temperature reaches 145F (63C), flipping halfway through.
5. Garnish with fresh parsley and serve immediately with lemon slices.

Nutrition:

Calories: 351   Carbohydrates: 3g
Fat: 18g   Fiber: 1g
Protein: 42g

72. Italian Sausages with Peppers and Onions

Preparation time: 5 minutes   **Cooking time:** 28 minutes   **Servings:** 3

Ingredients:

- 1 medium onion, thinly sliced
- 1 yellow or orange bell pepper
- 1 red bell pepper, thinly sliced
- ¼ cup avocado oil or melted coconut oil
- 1 teaspoon fine sea salt
- 6 Italian sausages
- Dijon mustard, for serving (optional)

Directions:

1. Preheat the air fryer to 400F (204C).
2. Place the onion and peppers in a large bowl. Drizzle with the oil and toss well to coat the veggies. Season with the salt.
3. Place the onion and peppers in a pie pan and cook in the air fryer for 8 minutes, stirring halfway through. Detach from the air fryer and set aside.
4. Spray the air fryer basket with avocado oil. Put the sausages in the air fryer basket and air fry for 20 minutes, or until crispy and golden brown
5. Place the onion and peppers on a serving platter and arrange the sausages on top. Serve Dijon mustard on the side, if desired.

Nutrition:

Calories: 576   Carbohydrates: 8g
Fat: 49g   Fiber: 2g
Protein: 25g

73. Pork Tenderloin with Avocado Lime Sauce

Preparation time: 10 minutes   **Cooking time:** 15 minutes   **Servings:** 4

Ingredients:

Marinade:

- ½ cup lime juice
- Grated zest of 1 lime
- 2 teaspoons stevia glyceride, or ¼ teaspoon liquid stevia
- 3 cloves garlic, minced
- 1½ teaspoons fine sea salt
- 1 teaspoon chili powder, or more for more heat
- 1 teaspoon smoked paprika
- 1 pound (454 g) pork tenderloin

Avocado Lime Sauce:

- 1 medium-sized ripe avocado, roughly chopped
- ½ cup full-fat sour cream (or coconut cream for dairy-free)
- Grated zest of 1 lime
- Juice of 1 lime
- 2 cloves garlic, roughly chopped
- ½ teaspoon fine sea salt
- ¼ teaspoon ground black pepper
- Chopped fresh cilantro leaves, for garnish
- Lime slices, for serving
- Pico de Gallo, for serving

Directions:
1. In a medium-sized casserole dish, stir together all the marinade ingredients until well combined. Add the tenderloin and coat it well in the marinade. Secure and place in the fridge to marinate for 2 hours or overnight.
2. Spray the air fryer basket with avocado oil. Preheat the air fryer to 400F (204C).
3. Detach the pork from the marinade and place it in the air fryer basket. Air fry for 13 to 15 minutes, until the internal temperature of the pork is 145F (63C), flipping after 7 minutes. Detach the pork from the air fryer and place it on a cutting board. Allow it to rest for 8 to 10 minutes, then cut it into ½-inch-thick slices.
4. While the pork cooks, make the avocado lime sauce: Place all the sauce ingredients in a food processor and purée until smooth.
5. Place the pork slices on a serving platter and spoon the avocado lime sauce on top. Brush with cilantro leaves and serve with lime slices and Pico de Gallo.

Nutrition:
Calories: 326

Fat: 19g

Protein: 26g

Carbohydrates: 15g

Fiber: 6g

74. Marinated Steak Tips with Mushrooms
Preparation time: 10 minutes   **Cooking time:** 10 minutes   **Servings:** 4

Ingredients:
- 1½ pounds (680 g) sirloin, trimmed and cut into 1-inch pieces
- 8 ounces (227 g) brown mushrooms, halved
- ¼ cup Worcestershire sauce
- 1 tablespoon Dijon mustard
- 1 tablespoon olive oil
- 1 teaspoon paprika
- 1 teaspoon crushed red pepper flakes
- 2 tablespoons chopped fresh parsley (optional)

Directions:
1. Place the beef and mushrooms in a gallon-size resealable bag. In a small bowl, whisk together the Worcestershire, mustard, olive oil, paprika, and red pepper flakes. Set the marinade into the bag and massage gently to ensure the beef and mushrooms are evenly coated. Secure the bag and refrigerate for at least 4 hours, preferably overnight. Remove from the refrigerator 30 minutes before cooking.
2. Preheat the air fryer to 400F (204C).
3. Drain and discard the marinade. Arrange the steak and mushrooms in the air fryer basket. Air fry for 10 minutes. Transfer to a serving plate and top with the parsley, if desired.

Nutrition:
Calories: 330

Fat: 17g

Protein: 41g

Carbohydrates: 2g

Fiber: 0g

75. Italian-Style Pork Chops
Preparation time: 5 minutes   **Cooking time:** 20 to 25 minutes   **Servings:** 4

Ingredients:
- 4 thick center-cut boneless pork chops (about 1½ pounds / 680 g)
- 1 tablespoon olive oil
- 1 teaspoon salt
- 1 (15 ounce / 425-g) can crushed tomatoes
- 1 tablespoon Italian seasoning
- 2 cloves garlic, minced
- ¼ cup chopped kalamata olives
- 2 tablespoons chopped fresh parsley

Directions:
1. Preheat the air fryer to 400F (204C).
2. Arrange the pork chops in a round baking dish. Drizzle with the olive oil and season both sides with the salt.

3. In a bowl, combine the tomatoes, Italian seasoning, and garlic. Pour the tomato mixture over the pork chops.
4. Air fry for 20 to 25 minutes. Remove the chops from the sauce and let rest for 5 minutes. Stir the olives and parsley into the sauce before serving with the pork chops.

Nutrition:
Calories: 350
Fat: 17g
Protein: 40g
Carbohydrates: 9g
Fiber: 2g

76. Rosemary Roast Beef

Preparation time: 5 minutes   **Cooking time:** 30 to 35 minutes   **Servings:** 8

Ingredients:
- 1 (2-pound / 907-g) top round beef roast, tied with kitchen string
- Sea salt and freshly ground black pepper
- 2 teaspoons minced garlic
- 2 tablespoons finely chopped fresh rosemary
- ¼ cup avocado oil

Directions:
1. Flavor the roast generously with salt and pepper.
2. In a small bowl, set together the garlic, rosemary, and avocado oil. Rub this all over the roast. Secure loosely with aluminum foil or plastic wrap and refrigerate for at least 12 hours or up to 2 days.
3. Detach the roast from the refrigerator and allow to sit at room temperature for about 1 hour.
4. Set the air fryer to 325F (163C). Set the roast in the air fryer basket and roast for 15 minutes. Flip the roast and cook for 15 to 20 minutes more, until the meat is browned and an instant-read thermometer reads 120F (49C) at the thickest part (for medium-rare).
5. Set the meat to a cutting board, and let it rest for 15 minutes before thinly slicing and serving.

Nutrition:
Calories: 213
Fat: 10g
Protein: 25g
Carbohydrates: 2g
Fiber: 1g

77. Tenderloin with Crispy Shallots

Preparation time: 5 minutes   **Cooking time:** 18 to 20 minutes   **Servings:** 6

Ingredients:
- 1½ pounds (680 g) beef tenderloin steaks
- Sea salt and freshly ground black pepper
- 4 medium shallots
- 1 teaspoon olive oil or avocado oil

Directions:
1. Flavor both sides of the steaks with salt and pepper and let them sit at room temperature for 45 minutes.
2. Set the air fryer to 400F (204C) and let it preheat for 5 minutes.
3. Working in batches, if necessary, place the steaks in the air fryer basket in a single layer and air fry for 5 minutes. Flip and cook for 5 minutes longer, until an instant-read thermometer inserted in the center of the steaks registers 120F (49C) for medium-rare (or as desired). Detach the steaks and tent with aluminum foil to rest.
4. Set the air fryer to 300F (149C). In a medium bowl, set the shallots with the oil. Place the shallots in the basket and air fry for 5 minutes, then give them a set and cook for 3 to 5 minutes more, until crispy and golden brown.
5. Place the steaks on serving plates and arrange the shallots on top.

Nutrition:
Calories: 186
Fat: 5g
Protein: 30g
Carbohydrates: 5g
Fiber: 0g

78. Sesame Beef Lettuce Tacos

Preparation time: 15 minutes   **Cooking time:** 8 to 10 minutes   **Servings:** 4

Ingredients:
- ¼ cup coconut aminos
- ¼ cup avocado oil
- 2 tablespoons cooking sherry
- 1 tablespoon Swerve
- 1 tablespoon ground cumin
- 1 teaspoon minced garlic
- Sea salt and freshly ground black pepper
- 1 pound (454 g) flank steak

- 8 butter lettuce leaves
- 2 scallions, sliced
- 1 tablespoon toasted sesame seeds
- Hot sauce, for serving
- Lime wedges, for serving
- Flaky sea salt (optional)

Directions:
1. In a small bowl, set together the coconut aminos, avocado oil, cooking sherry, Swerve, cumin, garlic, and salt and pepper to taste.
2. Place the steak in a shallow dish. Pour the marinade over the beef. Secure the dish with plastic wrap and let it marinate in the refrigerator for at least 2 hours or overnight.
3. Remove the flank steak from the dish and discard the marinade.
4. Set the air fryer to 400F (204C). Set the steak in the air fryer basket and air fry for 4 to 6 minutes. Flip the steak and cook until an instant-read thermometer reads 120F (49C) at the thickest part (or cook it to your desired doneness). Allow the steak to rest for 10 minutes, then slice it thinly against the grain.
5. Set 2 lettuce leaves on top of each other and add some sliced meat. Top with scallions and sesame seeds. Drizzle with hot sauce and lime juice, and finish with a little flaky salt (if using). Repeat with the remaining lettuce leaves and fillings.

Nutrition:
Calories: 349
Fat: 22g
Protein: 25g

Carbohydrates: 10g
Fiber: 5g

79. Chipotle Taco Pizzas

Preparation time: 25 minutes   **Cooking time:** 36 minutes   **Servings:** 6
Ingredients:

- 1 recipe Fathead Pizza Dough
- 1 pound (454 g) ground beef
- 2 tablespoons Taco Seasoning
- 1 canned chipotle chili in adobo sauce
- ⅓ cup plus 1 tablespoon sugar-free salsa, divided
- 6 ounces (170 g) Cheddar cheese, grated
- 3 scallions, chopped
- ¼ cup sour cream

Directions:
1. Divide the dough into three equal pieces. Set each piece between two sheets of parchment paper and roll it into a 7-inch round. et one dough round in a cake pan or air fryer pizza pan. Place the pan in the air fryer basket.
2. Set your air fryer to 375F (191C). Bake the dough for 6 minutes. Detach from the air fryer and repeat with the remaining dough.
3. While the crusts are cooking, heat a large skillet over medium-high heat. Attach the ground beef and cook, breaking the meat up with a spoon, for 5 minutes. Stir in the taco seasoning and chipotle chili and cook until the meat is browned. Remove the skillet from the heat and stir in ⅓ cup of salsa.
4. Divide the meat among the pizza crusts. Top with the cheese and scallions. Return one pizza to the air fryer and bake for 6 minutes, until the cheese is melted. Repeat with the remaining pizzas.
5. Combine the sour cream and remaining 1 tablespoon of salsa in a small bowl. Drizzle this over the finished pizzas.
6. If desired, top the pizzas with additional desired toppings, such as shredded romaine lettuce, pickled jalapeño slices, diced tomatoes, cilantro, and lime juice. Serve warm.

Nutrition:
Calories: 614
Fat: 52g
Protein: 34g

Carbohydrates: 10g
Fiber: 4g

80. Smoked Beef Mix

Preparation time: 5 minutes   **Cooking time:** 20 minutes   **Servings:** 4
Ingredients:

- 1pound beef stew meat, roughly cubed
- 1 tablespoon smoked paprika
- ½ cup beef stock
- ½ teaspoon garam masala
- 2 tablespoons olive oil
- A pinch of salt and black pepper

Directions:

1. Toss the beef with the smoked paprika and the other ingredients in the air fryer basket, toss, and cook for 20 minutes on each side at 390F. Serve by dividing the mixture between plates.

Nutrition:

Calories: 679

Fat: 53g

Protein: 42g

Carbohydrates: 3g

Fiber: 1g

Poultry

81. Duck Breasts with Red Wine and Orange Sauce

Preparation time: 10 minutes   **Cooking time:** 35 minutes   **Servings:** 4

Ingredients:

- ½ cup honey
- 2 cups orange juice
- 4 cups red wine
- 2 tablespoons sherry vinegar
- 2 cups chicken stock
- 2 teaspoons pumpkin pie spice
- 2 tablespoons butter
- 2 duck breasts, skin on and halved
- 2 tablespoons olive oil
- Salt and black pepper to the taste

Directions:

1. Warmth up a pan with the orange juice over medium heat, add honey, stir well and cook for 10 minutes.
2. Add wine, vinegar, stock, pie spice and butter, stir well, cook for 10 minutes more and take off heat.
3. Season duck breasts with salt and pepper, rub with olive oil, place in preheated air fryer at 370F and cook for 7 minutes on each side.
4. Divide duck breasts on plates, drizzle wine and orange juice all over and serve right away.
5. Enjoy!

Nutrition:

Calories: 300

Fat: 8g

Fiber: 12g

Carbohydrates: 24g

Protein: 11g

82. Duck Breast with Fig Sauce

Preparation time: 10 minutes   **Cooking time:** 20 minutes   **Servings:** 4

Ingredients:

- 2 duck breasts, skin on, halved
- 1 tablespoon olive oil
- ½ teaspoon thyme, chopped
- ½ teaspoon garlic powder
- ¼ teaspoon sweet paprika
- Salt and black pepper to the taste
- 1 cup beef stock
- 3 tablespoons butter, melted
- 1 shallot, chopped
- ½ cup port wine
- 4 tablespoons fig preserves
- 1 tablespoon almond flour

Directions:

1. Season duck breasts with salt and pepper, drizzle half of the melted butter, rub well, put in your air fryer's basket and set at 350F for 5 minutes on each side.
2. Meanwhile, heat up a pan with the olive oil and the rest of the butter over medium high heat, add shallot, stir and cook for 2 minutes.
3. Add thyme, garlic powder, paprika, stock, salt, pepper, wine and figs, stir and cook for 7-8 minutes.
4. Add flour, stir well, cook until sauce thickens a bit and take off heat.
5. Divide duck breasts on plates, drizzle figs sauce all over and serve. Enjoy!

Nutrition:

Calories: 246

Fat: 12g

Fiber: 4g

Carbohydrates: 22g

Protein: 3g

83. Duck Breasts and Raspberry Sauce

Preparation time: 10 minutes   **Cooking time:** 15 minutes   **Servings:** 4

Ingredients:

- 2 duck breasts skin on and scored
- Salt and black pepper to the taste
- Cooking spray
- ½ teaspoon cinnamon powder
- ½ cup raspberries
- 1 tablespoon Erythritol
- 1 teaspoon red wine vinegar
- ½ cup water

Directions:

1. Flavor the duck breasts with salt and pepper, spray them with cooking spray, put in preheated air fryer skin side down and cook at 350F for 10 minutes.
2. Heat up a pan with the water over medium heat, add raspberries, cinnamon, Erythritol and wine, stir, bring to a simmer, and transfer to your blender, puree and return to pan.
3. Add air fryer duck breasts to pan as well, toss to coat, divide among plates and serve right away.
4. Enjoy!

Nutrition:

Calories: 456

Carbohydrates: 14g

Fat: 22g

Protein: 45g

Fiber: 4g

84. Duck and Cherries

Preparation time: 10 minutes　　**Cooking time:** 20 minutes　　**Servings:** 4

Ingredients:

- ½ cup Erythritol
- ¼ cup honey
- ⅓ cup balsamic vinegar
- 1 teaspoon garlic, minced
- 1 tablespoon ginger, grated
- 1 teaspoon cumin, ground
- ½ teaspoon clove, ground
- ½ teaspoon cinnamon powder

- 4 sage leaves, chopped
- 1 jalapeno, chopped
- 2 cups rhubarb, sliced
- ½ cup yellow onion, chopped
- 2 cups cherries, pitted
- 3 duck breasts, boneless, skin on and scored
- Salt and black pepper to the taste

Directions:

1. Season duck breast with salt and pepper, put in your air fryer and cook at 350F for 5 minutes on each side.
2. Meanwhile, heat up a pan over medium heat, add Erythritol, honey, vinegar, garlic, ginger, cumin, clove, cinnamon, sage, jalapeno, rhubarb, onion and cherries, stir, bring to a simmer and cook for 10 minutes.
3. Add duck breasts, toss well, divide everything on plates and serve. Enjoy!

Nutrition:

Calories: 456

Carbohydrates: 64g

Fat: 13g

Protein: 31g

Fiber: 4g

85. Easy Duck Breasts

Preparation time: 10 minutes　　**Cooking time:** 15 minutes　　**Servings:** 4

Ingredients:

- 4 duck breasts, skinless and boneless
- 4 garlic heads, peeled, tops cut off and quartered
- 2 tablespoons lemon juice

- Salt and black pepper to the taste
- ½ teaspoon lemon pepper
- 1 and ½ tablespoon olive oil

Directions:

1. In a bowl, mix duck breasts with garlic, lemon juice, salt, pepper, lemon pepper and olive oil and toss everything.
2. Transfer duck and garlic to your air fryer and cook at 350F for 15 minutes.
3. Divide duck breasts and garlic on plates and serve.
4. Enjoy!

Nutrition:

Calories: 200

Carbohydrates: 11g

Fat: 7g

Protein: 17g

Fiber: 1g

86. Jerk Chicken Wings

Preparation time: 10 minutes　　**Cooking time:** 15 minutes　　**Servings:** 6-8

Ingredients:

- 1 tsp. salt
- ½ cup red wine vinegar
- 5 tbsp. lime juice

- 4 chopped scallions
- 1 tbsp. grated ginger
- 2 tbsp. brown Erythritol

- 1 tbsp. chopped thyme
- 1 tsp. white pepper
- 1 tsp. cayenne pepper
- 1 tsp. cinnamon
- 1 tbsp. allspice

- 1 Habanero pepper (seeds/ribs removed and chopped finely)
- 6 chopped garlic cloves
- 2 tbsp. low-sodium soy sauce
- 2 tbsp. olive oil
- 4 pounds of chicken wings

Directions:
1. Combine all ingredients except wings in a bowl. Pour into a gallon bag and add chicken wings. Chill 2-24 hours to marinate.
2. Ensure your air fryer is preheated to 390 degrees.
3. Place chicken wings into a strainer to drain excess liquids.
4. Pour half of the wings into your air fryer and cook 14-16 minutes, making sure to shake halfway through the cooking process.
5. Remove and repeat the process with remaining wings.

Nutrition:
Calories: 260

Carbohydrates: 4g

Fat: 7g

Proteins: 21g

87. Chicken Fajita Rollups

Preparation time: 10 minutes   **Cooking time:** 15 minutes   **Servings:** 6-8

Ingredients:

- ½ tsp. oregano
- ½ tsp. cayenne pepper
- 1 tsp. cumin
- 1 tsp. garlic powder
- 2 tsp. paprika

- ½ sliced red onion
- ½ yellow bell pepper
- ½ green bell pepper
- ½ red bell pepper, sliced into strips
- 3 chicken breasts

Directions:
1. Mix oregano, cayenne pepper, garlic powder, cumin and paprika along with a pinch or two of pepper and salt. Set to the side.
2. Slice chicken breasts lengthwise into 2 slices.
3. Between two pieces of parchment paper, add breast slices and pound till they are ¼-inch thick. With seasoning, liberally season both sides of chicken slices.
4. Put 2 strips of each color of bell pepper and a few onion slices onto chicken pieces.
5. Roll up tightly and secure with toothpicks.
6. Repeat with remaining ingredients and sprinkle and rub mixture that is left over the chicken rolls.
7. Lightly grease your air fryer basket and place 3 rollups into the fryer. Cook 12 minutes at 400 degrees.
8. Repeat with remaining rollups.
9. Serve with salad!

Nutrition:
Calories: 301

Carbohydrates: 23g

Fat: 6g

Proteins: 13g

88. Chicken Parmesan with Sauce

Preparation time: 10 minutes   **Cooking time:** 10 minutes   **Servings:** 2

Ingredients:

- 1 boneless skinless chicken breasts, sliced and half
- ½ cup panko breadcrumbs
- ¼ cup Parmesan cheese
- ¼ cup mozzarella cheese
- 1 egg, beaten

- ½ cup marinara sauce
- Dash of Italian seasoning
- Dash of salt
- Dash of pepper

Directions:
1. Heat fryer to 400 degrees. Spray basket with a small coating of cooking spray.
2. Slice the chicken breast horizontally. Place pieces between sheets of plastic wrap and pound until thin.

3. Merge breadcrumbs with the Parmesan cheese and seasonings. Mix well and set aside.
4. In a separate bowl, dip the chicken pieces in the egg. Then dredge in the breadcrumb mixture.
5. Set the chicken pieces in the air fryer, and lightly coat the tops with cooking spray. Cook for about 7 minutes.
6. Next, top with sauce and then a layer of the mozzarella cheese.
7. Cook for 3 more minutes, or until the cheese has melted. Serve.

Nutrition:

Calories: 270   Carbohydrates: 22g

Fat: 3g   Proteins: 21g

89. Chicken Croquettes

Preparation time: 10 minutes   **Cooking time:** 15 minutes   **Servings:** 2

Ingredients:

- ½ cup turkey or chicken, cooked, chopped
- 1 cup prepared stuffing
- 1 egg
- 3 Tbsp. glucomannan powder
- ⅔ cup turkey or chicken gravy
- ¼ cup cranberry sauce
- ½ cup panko breadcrumbs

Directions:

1. Preheat air fryer to 380 degrees.
2. Take about 2 tablespoons of the leftover turkey or chicken, roll into a ball and surround it with about 2 tablespoons of stuffing. Roll into balls. Repeat with remaining chicken and stuffing.
3. In a bowl, beat the egg. In another bowl, attach the glucomannan powder and in a third bowl, all the panko breadcrumbs.
4. Roll the chicken/turkey ball in the glucomannan powder, then dip into the egg mixture. Finally, dredge in the breadcrumbs and set aside. Repeat the process with the remaining balls.
5. Set your air fryer basket with oil and spritz additional oil on each croquette. Put as many croquettes in the basket without touching and cook for 6 minutes. Bend and cook for about 4 more minutes, or until fully browned on all sides.
6. Dip cooked croquettes in gravy and serve with cranberry sauce.

Nutrition:

Calories: 239   Carb: 1823g

Fat: 10g   Proteins: 12g

90. Chicken Tenders

Preparation time: 35 minutes   **Cooking time:** 10 minutes   **Servings:** 2

Ingredients:

- ½ lb. chicken meat, cut into about 5-8 chicken tenders
- ⅔ cup buttermilk
- ¼ cup almond flour
- ⅛ tsp. baking powder
- ⅔ cup panko breadcrumbs
- 2 Tbsp. butter, melted
- Dash of salt and pepper
- ¼ tsp. celery salt
- Dash oregano
- Dash cayenne pepper
- Dash thyme
- ½ tsp. paprika

Directions:

1. Cut chicken into tender sized pieces. Set in a zippered storage bag with the buttermilk. Seal the bag and marinate for at least one half hour. Ideally, the chicken would marinade in the buttermilk for several hours.
2. When ready, preheat the air fryer to 350 degrees.
3. In a bowl, combine the flour, baking powder, spices and breadcrumbs.
4. Take chicken strips from the marinade one at a time. Dredge in breadcrumb mixture, coating both sides.
5. Place prepared chicken strips in the air fryer and cook for 4 minutes. Brush chicken with melted butter, flip and cook for an additional 6 to 8 minutes until they are a crispy golden brown. The internal temperature should reach 175 degrees.

Nutrition:

Calories: 221   Fiber: 2g   Protein: 14

Fat: 12g   Carbohydrates: 5g

91. Cornish Game Hens

Preparation time: 5 minutes   **Cooking time:** 30 minutes   **Servings:** 2

Ingredients:

- 2 cup Cornish game hens
- 2 small onions
- 3 Tbsp. olive oil
- 2 tsp. garlic salt
- Salt and pepper to taste

Directions:

1. Preheat air fryer to 390 degrees.
2. Remove gizzards from the hens. Rub the skin with olive oil.
3. Combine salt, pepper and garlic salt. Rub the mixture over the skin of the hens.
4. Peel the onions and put them in the cavities of the Cornish game hens, and the tie the legs together with kitchen twine.
5. Lightly set the fryer basket with cooking spray and place the hens in the basket, breast side up.
6. Cook for about 25 minutes.
7. When cooked, remove. Allow to sit before serving.

Nutrition:

Calories: 340

Fat: 25.5g

Fiber: 3.2g

Carbohydrates: 8.2g

Protein: 20.5g

92. Sriacha Chicken Wings

Preparation time: 5 minutes   **Cooking time:** 30 minutes   **Servings:** 2

Ingredients:

- 14-16 party chicken wings (with tips removed)
- ⅓ cup honey
- 2 Tbsp. sriracha sauce
- 4 tsp. soy sauce
- 1 Tbsp. butter
- 3 Tbsp. lime juice
- Salt and pepper to taste

Directions:

1. Preheat air fryer to 360 degrees. Wash wings and pat dry with a paper towel, then spray lightly with cooking spray. Sprinkle with salt and pepper. Air fry for a half hour, turning every 7-8 minutes.
2. In the meantime, combine lime juice, sriracha sauce, soy sauce, honey and butter in a small sauce pot. Cook until it comes to a boil, stirring frequently. Boil for three minutes and remove from heat.
3. When the chicken wings are ready, remove from the air pot and add to a bowl. While still hot, toss with the sriracha sauce and serve.

Nutrition:

Calories: 220

Fat: 14g

Fiber: 2g

Carbohydrates: 5g

Protein: 12g

93. Rotisserie Chicken

Preparation time: 4 minutes   **Cooking time:** 25 minutes   **Servings:** 2

Ingredients:

- 1 whole fryer chicken, 3-4 pounds
- 2 Tbsp. olive oil
- 2 tsp. seasoning salt
- ¼ tsp. garlic powder
- ¼ tsp. onion powder
- ⅛ tsp. turmeric
- Pinch of glucomannan powder

Directions:

1. Preheat the air fryer to 350 degrees.
2. Combine the seasoning salt, garlic powder, onion powder, turmeric and glucomannan powder. Mix well and set aside.
3. Set the chicken by removing any giblets and dry with a paper towel. Rub olive oil onto the chicken and coat with the seasoning.

4. Turn the chicken upside down and place it, breast side down, in the air fryer. Fry for a half hour at 350 degrees. Then bend the chicken over and air fry for another 30 minutes. Remove when internal temperature is 165 degrees. Let chicken rest for 8 to 10 minutes and serve.

Nutrition:

Calories: 180

Fat: 3g

Carbohydrates: 10g

Proteins: 9g

94. Herb Wings

Preparation time: 10 minutes   **Cooking time:** 15 minutes   **Servings:** 4

Ingredients:

- 2 lbs. chicken wings
- 1 tsp. paprika
- ½ cup parmesan cheese, grated
- 1 tsp. herb de Provence
- Salt

Directions:

1. In a small bowl, mix cheese, herb de Provence, paprika, and salt.
2. Coat chicken wings with cheese mixture.
3. Select Air Fry mode.
4. Set time to 15 minutes and temperature 350F then press START.
5. The air fryer display will prompt you to ADD FOOD once the temperature is reached then set chicken wings in the air fryer basket.
6. Serve and enjoy.

Nutrition:

Calories: 200

Fat: 6g

Carbohydrates: 19g

Proteins: 21g

95. Chicken and Mushroom Kebabs

Preparation time: 10 minutes   **Cooking time:** 23 minutes   **Servings:** 2

Ingredients:

- 2 boneless skinless chicken breasts
- ¼ cup honey
- ⅓ cup soy sauce
- 1 Tbsp. sesame seeds
- 2 bell peppers, diced in 1-inch pieces
- 1 cup mushrooms
- 1 summer squash, diced in 1-inch pieces
- Olive oil or other cooking spray
- Salt and pepper to taste

Directions:

1. Soak bamboo skewers in water and preheat air fryer to 325 degrees.
2. Divide chicken into 1 inch cubes. Set with oil and season with salt and pepper.
3. Combine honey, sesame seeds and soy sauce, stirring well.
4. Assemble skewers with chicken and cut up vegetables. Coat with the honey sauce and put in the air fryer basket.
5. Air fry for 10 minutes. Brush with honey mixture again and cook for a remaining 5 to 10 minutes.

Nutrition:

Calories: 270

Fat: 3g

Carbohydrates: 22g

Proteins: 21g

96. Sweet and Tangy Chicken Wings

Preparation time: 10 minutes   **Cooking time:** 23 minutes   **Servings:** 2

Ingredients:

- 2 Tbsp. honey
- 2 Tbsp. lemon juice
- 2 Tbsp. soy sauce
- Salt and pepper to taste

Directions:

1. Rinse wings and pat dry with a paper towel. Combine remaining ingredients, stirring well. Add the marinade in a plastic sealable storage bag along with the chicken wings.
2. Let marinade for at least 6 hours, preferably a full day.
3. When ready to bake, remove the chicken and let them come to room temperature, about a half hour.
4. In the meantime, preheat the air fryer to 350 degrees.

5. Remove chicken from marinade and put in the air fryer. Cook for 6 minutes, and then flip over. Cook for an additional 3 minutes, watching carefully that they don't burn because of the honey in the coating.
6. Serve immediately.

Nutrition:

Calories: 250

Fat: 12g

Carbohydrates: 12g

Proteins: 20g

97. Chicken Nachos

Preparation time: 10 minutes   **Cooking time:** 30 minutes   **Servings:** 4

Ingredients:

- 2 medium tomatoes, seeded and diced
- 15 oz. can black beans
- 1 tsp. garlic powder
- 1 tsp. salt
- 4 scallions, chopped
- ¾ cup chopped fresh cilantro
- 8-oz. shredded cheese, Mexican blend
- 2 tsp. chili powder
- 2 tsp. ground cumin
- 2 cups chopped or shredded cooked chicken breasts
- Tortilla chips
- 1 jalapeño, chopped

Directions:

1. Combine the chili powder, garlic powder, cumin, and salt in a small bowl.
2. Add the chicken into the mixture and toss evenly to coat.
3. Line the Air Fryer basket with aluminum foil. Arrange the chips inside the Air Fryer basket and top with the chicken, beans, tomatoes, scallion, and cheese.
4. Set the Air Fryer to 300F and bake for 15 minutes. Garnish with cilantro and jalapeño.

Nutrition:

Calories: 239

Fat: 10g

Carb: 1823g

Proteins: 12g

98. Turkey Breast

Preparation time: 10 minutes   **Cooking time:** 60 minutes   **Servings:** 4

Ingredients:

- 4 tbsp. butter
- Ground pepper
- 2 tbsp. olive oil
- ¼ tsp. ground cumin
- 1 tsp. Worcestershire sauce
- A handful of sage, chopped
- 1 lb. turkey breast steaks, pound and slice to pieces
- Kosher salt
- 1 tbsp. fresh lemon juice
- ¼ cup chives, chopped

Directions:

1. Oil the Air Fryer basket and set the temperature of the Air Fryer to 350F.
2. Season the turkey with pepper and salt.
3. Pulse the cumin, lemon juice, salt, sauce, chives, and salt in a blender.
4. Airs fry the turkey and serve with the chives mixture.

Nutrition:

Carbohydrates: 19g

Proteins: 16g

Calories: 261

Fat: 8g

99. Glazed Rosemary Chicken

Preparation time: 10 minutes   **Cooking time:** 20 minutes   **Servings:** 2

Ingredients:

- 1 spring rosemary, roughly chopped
- ½ tsp. red pepper flakes
- 2 tsp. honey
- 2 chicken breasts, rinsed and pat dry
- 1 tsp. olive oil
- ground pepper, to taste
- kosher salt, to taste

Directions:

1. Brush the chicken with olive oil. Season the chicken (skin-side up) with pepper, salt, red pepper, honey, and rosemary.
2. Preheat the Air Fryer to 330F and bake the chicken for 15 minutes, until tender.

Nutrition:

Calories: 280

Fat: 14g

Fiber: 3g

Carbohydrates: 5g

Protein: 14g

100.   Air Fried Butter Milk Chicken

Preparation time: 10 minutes   **Cooking time:** 8 hours 20 minutes   **Servings:** 4

Ingredients:

- 2 chicken breasts

Marinade:

- 2 cups buttermilk
- 2 tsp. salt

- 2 tsp. black pepper
- 1 tsp. cayenne pepper

Seasoned Flour:

- 2 cups almond flour
- 1 tbsp. baking powder
- 1 tbsp. garlic powder

- 1 tbsp. paprika powder
- 1 tsp. salt
- 1 tsp. pepper

Directions:

1. To prepare the marinade, combine the pepper, salt, and chicken pieces in a large bowl. Add the buttermilk and refrigerate for at least 8 hours.
2. In another separate large bowl, mix the flour, paprika, salt, pepper, baking powder, and garlic powder. Take out the marinated chicken and discard the marinade. Coat the marinated chicken with the seasoned flour mixture.
3. Transfer the coated chicken into the Air Fryer basket and cook in a 370F preheated oil-coated Air Fryer.
4. Cook the chicken for about 30 minutes and spray cooking oil at intervals.
5. Serve.

Nutrition:

Calories: 160

Fat: 4g

Fiber: 2g

Carbohydrates: 8g

Protein: 8g

Fish and Sea food

101. Garlic Shrimp Mix

Preparation time: 10 minutes   **Cooking time:** 5 minutes   **Servings:** 3

Ingredients:

- 1-pound shrimps, peeled
- ½ teaspoon garlic powder
- ¼ teaspoon minced garlic
- 1 teaspoon ground cumin
- ¼ teaspoon lemon zest, grated
- ½ tablespoon avocado oil
- ½ teaspoon dried parsley

Directions:

1. In the mixing bowl mix up shrimps, garlic powder, minced garlic, ground cumin, lemon zest, and dried parsley. Then add avocado oil and mix up the shrimps well.
2. Preheat the air fryer to 400F.
3. Put the shrimps in the preheated air fryer basket and cook for 5 minutes.

Nutrition:

Calories: 187
Fat: 3g
Fiber: 0.2g
Carbohydrates: 3.2g
Protein: 34.7g

102. Tilapia and Tomato Salsa

Preparation time: 5 minutes   **Cooking time:** 15 minutes   **Servings:** 4

Ingredients:

- 4 tilapia fillets, boneless
- 1 tablespoon olive oil
- A pinch of salt and black pepper
- 12 ounces tomatoes, chopped
- 2 tablespoons green onions, chopped
- 2 tablespoons sweet red pepper, chopped
- 1 tablespoon balsamic vinegar

Directions:

1. Arrange the tilapia in a baking sheet that fits the air fryer and season with salt and pepper. In a bowl, merge all the other ingredients, toss and spread over the fish. Introduce the pan in the fryer and cook at 350F for 15 minutes.
2. Divide the mix between plates and serve.

Nutrition:

Calories: 221
Fat: 12g
Fiber: 2g
Carbohydrates: 5g
Protein: 14g

103. Crusted Turmeric Salmon

Preparation time: 15 minutes   **Cooking time:** 8 minutes   **Servings:** 4

Ingredients:

- 12 oz. salmon fillet
- ¼ cup pistachios, grinded
- 1 teaspoon cream cheese
- ½ teaspoon ground nutmeg
- 2 tablespoons coconut flour
- ½ teaspoon ground turmeric
- ¼ teaspoon sage
- ½ teaspoon salt
- 1 tablespoon heavy cream
- Cooking spray

Directions:

1. Cut the salmon fillet on 4 servings. In the mixing bowl mix up cream cheese, ground turmeric, sage, salt, and heavy cream. Then in the separated bowl mix up coconut flour and pistachios. Dip the salmon fillets in the cream cheese mixture and then coat in the pistachio mixture.
2. Preheat the air fryer to 380F. Place the coated salmon fillets in the air fryer and spray them with the cooking spray. Cook the fish for 8 minutes.

Nutrition:

Calories: 168
Fat: 9.5g
Fiber: 2g
Carbohydrates: 3.7g
Protein: 18.2g

104. Catfish with Spring Onions and Avocado

Preparation time: 5 minutes   **Cooking time:** 15 minutes   **Servings:** 4

Ingredients:

- 2 teaspoons oregano, dried
- 2 teaspoons cumin, ground
- 2 teaspoons sweet paprika
- A pinch of salt and black pepper
- 4 catfish fillets
- avocado, peeled and cubed
- ½ cup spring onions, chopped
- 2 tablespoons cilantro, chopped
- 2 teaspoons olive oil
- tablespoons lemon juice

Directions:

1. In a bowl, merge all the ingredients except the fish and toss. Arrange this in a baking pan that fits the air fryer, top with the fish, set the pan in the machine and cook at 360F for 15 minutes, flipping the fish halfway.
2. Divide between plates and serve.

Nutrition:

Calories: 280   Carbohydrates: 5g

Fat: 14g   Protein: 14g

Fiber: 3g

105. Ginger Cod

Preparation time: 10 minutes   **Cooking time:** 8 minutes   **Servings:** 2

Ingredients:

- 10 oz. cod fillet
- ½ teaspoon cayenne pepper
- ¼ teaspoon ground coriander
- ½ teaspoon ground ginger
- ½ teaspoon ground black pepper
- 1 tablespoon sunflower oil
- ½ teaspoon salt
- ½ teaspoon dried rosemary
- ½ teaspoon ground paprika

Directions:

1. In the shallow bowl mix up cayenne pepper, ground coriander, ginger, ground black pepper, salt, dried rosemary, and ground paprika. Then rub the cod fillet with the spice mixture. After this, sprinkle it with sunflower oil.
2. Preheat the air fryer to 390F.
3. Place the cod fillet in the air fryer and cook it for 4 minutes. Then carefully flip the fish on another side and cook for 4 minutes more.

Nutrition:

Calories: 183   Carbohydrates: 1.4g

Fat: 8.5g   Protein: 25.6g

Fiber: 0.7g

106. Paprika Tilapia

Preparation time: 5 minutes   **Cooking time:** 20 minutes   **Servings:** 4

Ingredients:

- 4 tilapia fillets, boneless
- 3 tablespoons ghee, melted
- A pinch of salt and black pepper
- 2 tablespoons capers
- ½ teaspoon garlic powder
- ½ teaspoon smoked paprika
- ½ teaspoon oregano, dried
- 2 tablespoons lemon juice

Directions:

1. In a bowl, merge all the ingredients except the fish and toss. Arrange the fish in a pan that fits the air fryer, pour the capers mix all over, put the pan in the air fryer and cook 360F for 20 minutes, shaking halfway.
2. Divide between plates and serve hot.

Nutrition:

Calories: 224   Carbohydrates: 2g

Fat: 10g   Protein: 18g

Fiber: 0g

107. Shrimp Skewers

Preparation time: 10 minutes **Cooking time:** 5 minutes **Servings:** 5

Ingredients:

- 4-pounds shrimps, peeled
- 2 tablespoons fresh cilantro, chopped
- 2 tablespoons apple cider vinegar
- 1 teaspoon ground coriander
- 1 tablespoon avocado oil
- Cooking spray

Directions:

1. In the shallow bowl mix up avocado oil, ground coriander, apple cider vinegar, and fresh cilantro. Then put the shrimps in the big bowl and sprinkle with avocado oil mixture.
2. Merge them well and leave for 10 minutes to marinate. After this, string the shrimps on the skewers.
3. Preheat the air fryer to 400F. Arrange the shrimp skewers in the air fryer and cook them for 5 minutes.

Nutrition:

Calories: 223

Fat: 14.9g

Fiber: 3.1g

Carbohydrates: 5.5g

Protein: 17.4g

108. Stevia Cod

Preparation time: 5 minutes **Cooking time:** 14 minutes **Servings:** 4

Ingredients:

- ⅓ cup stevia
- 2 tablespoons coconut aminos
- 4 cod fillets, boneless
- A pinch of salt and black pepper

Directions:

1. In a pan that fits the air fryer, combine all the ingredients and toss gently. Introduce the pan in the fryer and cook at 350F for 14 minutes, flipping the fish halfway.
2. Divide everything between plates and serve.

Nutrition:

Calories: 267

Fat: 18g

Fiber: 2g

Carbohydrates: 5g

Protein: 20g

109. Butter Crab Muffins

Preparation time: 15 minutes **Cooking time:** 20 minutes **Servings:** 2

Ingredients:

- 5 oz. crab meat, chopped
- 2 eggs, beaten
- 2 tablespoons almond flour
- ¼ teaspoon baking powder
- ½ teaspoon apple cider vinegar
- ½ teaspoon ground paprika
- 1 tablespoon butter, softened
- Cooking spray

Directions:

1. Grind the chopped crab meat and put it in the bowl. Add eggs, almond flour, baking powder, apple cider vinegar, ground paprika, and butter. Stir the mixture until homogenous. Preheat the air fryer to 365F.
2. Spray the muffin molds with cooking spray. Then pour the crab meat batter in the muffin molds and place them in the preheated air fryer.
3. Cook the crab muffins for 20 minutes or until they are light brown.
4. Cool the cooked muffins to the room temperature and remove from the muffin mold.

Nutrition:

Calories: 340

Fat: 25.5g

Fiber: 3.2g

Carbohydrates: 8.2g

Protein: 20.5g

110. Tilapia and Kale

Preparation time: 5 minutes **Cooking time:** 20 minutes **Servings:** 4

Ingredients:

- 4 tilapia fillets, boneless
- Salt and black pepper to the taste
- 2 garlic cloves, minced
- 1 teaspoon fennel seeds

- ½ teaspoon red pepper flakes, crushed
- 1 bunch kale, chopped
- Table9spoons olive oil

Directions:
1. In a pan that fits the fryer, combine all the ingredients, put the pan in the fryer and cook at 360F for 20 minutes.
2. Divide everything between plates and serve.

Nutrition:
Calories: 240
Fat: 12g
Fiber: 2g

Carbohydrates: 4g
Protein: 12g

111. Chili Haddock

Preparation time: 10 minutes | **Cooking time:** 8 minutes | **Servings:** 4

Ingredients:
- 12 oz. haddock fillet
- 1 egg, beaten
- 1 teaspoon cream cheese
- 1 teaspoon chili flakes
- ½ teaspoon salt
- 1 tablespoon flax meal
- Cooking spray

Directions:
1. Cut the haddock on 4 pieces and sprinkle with chili flakes and salt. After this, in the small bowl mix up egg and cream cheese. Dip the haddock pieces in the egg mixture and generously sprinkle with flax meal.
2. Preheat the air fryer to 400F.
3. Put the prepared haddock pieces in the air fryer in one layer and cook them for 4 minutes from each side or until they are golden brown.

Nutrition:
Calories: 122
Fat: 2g
Fiber: 0.5g

Carbohydrates: 0.6g
Protein: 22.5g

112. Lime Cod

Preparation time: 5 minutes | **Cooking time:** 14 minutes | **Servings:** 4

Ingredients:
- cod fillets, boneless
- 1 tablespoon olive oil
- Salt and black pepper to the taste
- 2 teaspoons sweet paprika
- Juice of 1 lime

Directions:
1. In a bowl, merge all the ingredients, transfer the fish to your air fryer's basket and cook 350F for 7 minutes on each side.
2. Divide the fish between plates and serve with a side salad.

Nutrition:
Calories: 240
Fat: 14g
Fiber: 2g

Carbohydrates: 4g
Protein: 16g

113. Mackerel with Spring Onions and Peppers

Preparation time: 15 minutes | **Cooking time:** 20 minutes | **Servings:** 5

Ingredients:
- 1-pound mackerel, trimmed
- 1 tablespoon ground paprika
- 1 green bell pepper
- ½ cup spring onions, chopped
- 1 tablespoon avocado oil
- 1 teaspoon apple cider vinegar
- ½ teaspoon salt

Directions:
1. Wash the mackerel if needed and sprinkle with ground paprika. Chop the green bell pepper. Then fill the mackerel with bell pepper and spring onion. After this, sprinkle the fish with avocado oil, apple cider vinegar, and salt.
2. Preheat the air fryer to 375F.

3. Place the mackerel in the air fryer basket and cook it for 20 minutes.

Nutrition:

Calories: 258

Fat: 16.8g

Fiber: 1.2g

Carbohydrates: 3.8g

Protein: 22.2g

114.   Ginger Salmon

Preparation time: 5 minutes   **Cooking time:** 12 minutes   **Servings:** 4

Ingredients:

- 2 tablespoons lime juice
- 1 pound salmon fillets, boneless, skinless and cubed
- 1 tablespoon ginger, grated
- 4 teaspoons olive oil
- 1 tablespoon coconut aminos
- 1 tablespoon sesame seeds, toasted
- 1 tablespoon chives, chopped

Directions:

1. In a pan that fits the air fryer, combine all the ingredients, toss, introduce in the fryer and cook at 360F for 12 minutes.
2. Divide into bowls and serve.

Nutrition:

Calories: 206

Fat: 8g

Fiber: 1g

Carbohydrates: 4g

Protein: 13g

115.   Sardine Cakes

Preparation time: 15 minutes   **Cooking time:** 10 minutes   **Servings:** 5

Ingredients:

- 12 oz. sardines, trimmed, cleaned
- ¼ cup coconut flour
- 1 egg, beaten
- 2 tablespoons flax meal
- 1 teaspoon ground black pepper
- 1 teaspoon salt
- Cooking spray

Directions:

1. Chop the sardines roughly and put them in the bowl. Add coconut flour, egg, flax meal, ground black pepper, and salt. Mix up the mixture with the help of the fork. Then make 5 cakes from the sardine mixture.
2. Preheat the air fryer to 390F.
3. Set the air fryer basket with cooking spray and place the cakes inside. Cook them for 5 minutes from each side.

Nutrition:

Calories: 170

Fat: 9.8g

Fiber: 1.2g

Carbohydrates: 1.5g

Protein: 18.6g

116.   Coconut Shrimp

Preparation time: 5 minutes   **Cooking time:** 12 minutes   **Servings:** 4

Ingredients:

- 1 tablespoon ghee, melted
- 1 pound shrimp, peeled and deveined
- ¼ cup coconut cream
- A pinch of red pepper flakes
- salt and black pepper
- 1 tablespoon parsley, chopped
- 1 tablespoon chives, chopped

Directions:

1. In a pan that fits the fryer, combine all the ingredients except the parsley, put the pan in the fryer and cook at 360F for 12 minutes.
2. Divide the mix into bowls, sprinkle the parsley on top and serve.

Nutrition:

Calories: 195

Fat: 11g

Fiber: 2g

Carbohydrates: 4g

Protein: 11g

117.   Halibut Steaks

Preparation time: 15 minutes   **Cooking time:** 10 minutes   **Servings:** 4

Ingredients:

- 24 oz. halibut steaks (6 oz. each fillet)
- ½ teaspoon salt
- ½ teaspoon ground black pepper
- 4 oz. bacon, sliced
- 1 tablespoon sunflower oil

Directions:

1. Cut every halibut fillet on 2 parts and sprinkle with salt and ground black pepper. Then wrap the fish fillets in the sliced bacon.
2. Preheat the air fryer to 400F.
3. Sprinkle the halibut bites with sunflower oil and put in the air fryer basket. Cook the meal for 5 minutes. Then flip the fish bites on another side and cook them for 5 minutes more.

Nutrition:

Calories: 375

Fat: 19.4g

Fiber: 0.1g

Carbohydrates: 0.6g

Protein: 46.5g

118.   Ham-Wrapped Prawns with Roasted Pepper Chutney

Preparation time: 15 minutes   **Cooking time:** 13 minutes   **Servings:** 4

Ingredients:

- 1 large red bell pepper
- 8 king prawns, peeled and deveined
- 4 ham slices, halved
- 1 garlic clove, minced
- 1 tablespoon olive oil
- ½ tablespoon paprika
- Salt and freshly ground black pepper

Directions:

1. Warmth the Air fryer to 375Fahrenheit and grease the Air fryer basket.
2. Cook for about 10 minutes in the Air fryer basket with the bell pepper. Put the bell pepper in a bowl and set aside for 15 minutes, sealed.
3. Detach the stems and seeds from the bell pepper before peeling and chopping it.
4. In a blender, combine the chopped bell pepper, garlic, paprika, and olive oil and pulse until a puree form.
5. Wrap each prawn in a ham slice and put in the Air fryer basket. Cook for 3 minutes and serve with roasted pepper chutney on the side.

Nutrition:

Calories: 267

Fat: 18g

Fiber: 2g

Carbohydrates: 5g

Protein: 20g

119.   Tuna Pie

Preparation time: 10 minutes   **Cooking time:** 30 minutes   **Servings:** 4

Ingredients:

- 2 hard-boiled eggs
- 2 tuna cans
- 200 ml fried tomato
- 1 sheet of broken dough.

Directions:

1. Break the eggs into tiny pieces and blend with the tuna and tomato in a mixing bowl.
2. Spread the split dough sheet out and cut it into two squares.
3. Place the tuna, eggs, and tomato mixture on one of the squares.
4. Cover with the other, join at the ends, and embellish with any remaining small bits. Preheat the air fryer to 180C for a few minutes.
5. Set the timer for 15 minutes at 180C in the air fryer basket.

Nutrition:

Calories: 70

Protein: 2g

Fiber: 3g

Fat: 4g

Sodium: 23mg

Carbohydrates: 8g

Sugar: 4g

120. Tuna Puff Pastry

Preparation time: 5 minutes   **Cooking time:** 15 minutes   **Servings:** 2

Ingredients:

- 2 square puff pastry dough, bought ready
- 1 egg (white and yolk separated)
- ½ cup tuna tea
- ½ cup chopped parsley tea
- ½ cup chopped tea olives
- Salt and pepper to taste

Directions:

1. Prepare the air fryer by preheating it. Set the timer for 5 minutes and the oven to 200F. Combine the tuna, olives, and parsley in a mixing dish. Flavor with salt and pepper to taste, then set aside.
2. Half of the filling should be put in each dough and folded in half. Close gently after brushing with egg white. Set two small cuts at the top of the air outlet after it has been closed. Brush with the yolk of an egg.
3. Put in the air fryer's basket. Click the power button and set the timer for 10 minutes.

Nutrition:

Calories: 160

Fat: 2g

Fiber: 5g

Carbohydrates: 10g

Protein: 8g

Vegetables

---

121. Traditional Indian Bhaji

Preparation time: 10 minutes **Cooking time:** 30 minutes **Servings:** 4

Ingredients:

- 2 eggs, beaten
- ½ cup almond meal
- ½ cup coconut flour
- ½ teaspoon baking powder
- 1 teaspoon curry paste
- 1 teaspoon cumin seed
- 1 teaspoon minced fresh ginger root
- Salt and black pepper, to your liking
- 2 red onions, chopped
- 1 Indian green chili, pureed
- Non-stick cooking spray

Directions:

1. Whisk the eggs, almond meal, coconut flour and baking powder in a mixing dish to make a thick batter; add in the cold water if needed.
2. Add in curry paste, cumin seeds, ginger root, salt, and black pepper.
3. Now, add onions and chili pepper; mix until everything is well incorporated.
4. Shape the balls and slightly press them to make the patties. Spritz the patties with cooking oil on all sides.
5. Set a sheet of aluminum foil in the Air Fryer food basket. Place the fritters on foil.
6. Then, air-fry them at 360F for 15 minutes; flip them over, press the power button and cook for another 20 minutes. Serve right away!

Nutrition:

Calories: 332

Fat: 13g

Fiber: 3g

Carbohydrates: 14g

Protein: 23g

---

122. Roasted Peppers with Greek Mayo Sauce

Preparation time: 10 minutes

Cooking time: 30 minutes

Servings: 4

Ingredients:

- 2 bell peppers, cut into strips
- 1 teaspoon avocado oil
- ½ teaspoon celery salt
- ¼ teaspoon red pepper flakes, crushed
- ½ cup mayonnaise
- 1 clove garlic, minced
- 1 teaspoon lemon juice

Directions:

1. Toss the peppers with avocado oil, celery salt, and red pepper flakes.
2. Air-fry them at 380F for 10 minutes. Shake the cooking basket and cook for 20 minutes more.
3. In the meantime, thoroughly combine the mayonnaise, garlic, and lemon juice.
4. When the peppers come out of the Air Fryer, check them for doneness. Serve with chilled mayonnaise sauce and enjoy!

Nutrition:

Calories: 120

Fat: 1g

Fiber: 4g

Carbohydrates: 8g

Protein: 15g

---

123. Vegetable Salsa Wraps

Preparation time: 10 minutes **Cooking time:** 10 minutes **Servings:** 4

Ingredients:

- 1 cup red onion, sliced
- 1 zucchini, chopped
- 1 poblano pepper, deveined and finely chopped
- 1 head lettuce
- ½ cup salsa (homemade or store-bought)
- 8 ounces mozzarella cheese

Directions:

1. Begin by preheating your Air Fryer to 390F.
2. Cook red onion, zucchini, and poblano pepper until they are tender and fragrant or about 7 minutes.

3. Divide the sautéed mixture among lettuce leaves; spoon the salsa over the top. Finish off with mozzarella cheese. Wrap lettuce leaves around the filling. Enjoy!

Nutrition:

Calories: 251   Sodium: 896mg

Protein: 10g   Carbohydrates: 8g

Fat: 21g   Sugar: 2g

124.   Mediterranean Falafel with Tzatziki

Preparation time: 10 minutes   **Cooking time:** 30 minutes   **Servings:** 4

Ingredients:

For the Falafel:

- 2 cups cauliflower, grated
- ¼ teaspoon baking powder
- ⅓ cup warm water

- ½ teaspoon salt
- 1 tablespoon coriander leaves, finely chopped
- 2 tablespoons fresh lemon juice

Vegan Tzatziki:

- 1 cup plain Greek yogurt
- 2 tablespoons lime juice, freshly squeezed
- ¼ teaspoon ground black pepper
- ⅓ teaspoon sea salt flakes

- 2 tablespoons extra-virgin olive oil
- 2 tablespoons chopped fresh dill
- 1 clove garlic, pressed
- ½ fresh cucumber, grated

Directions:

1. In a bowl, merge all the ingredients for the falafel. Allow the mixture to stay for approximately 10 minutes.
2. Now, air-fry at 390F for 15 minutes; make sure to flip them over halfway through the cooking time.
3. To make Greek tzatziki, blend all ingredients in your food processor.
4. Serve warm falafel with chilled tzatziki. Enjoy!

Nutrition:

Calories: 240   Carbohydrates: 5g

Fat: 12g   Protein: 11g

Fiber: 2g

125.   Veggie Fingers with Monterey Jack Cheese

Preparation time: 10 minutes   **Cooking time:** 10 minutes   **Servings:** 4

Ingredients:

- 10 ounces cauliflower
- ¼ cup almond flour
- 1 ½ teaspoons soy sauce
- Salt and freshly ground black pepper

- 1 teaspoon cayenne pepper
- 1 cup parmesan cheese, grated
- ¾ teaspoon dried dill weed
- 1 tablespoon olive oil

Directions:

1. Firstly, pulse the cauliflower in your food processor; transfer them to a bowl and add ¼ cup almond flour, soy sauce, salt, black pepper, and cayenne pepper.
2. Roll the mixture into veggie fingers shape. In another bowl, place grated parmesan cheese and dried dill.
3. Now, coat the veggie fingers with the parmesan mixture, covering completely. Drizzle veggie fingers with olive oil.
4. Air-fry for 15 minutes at 350F; turn them over once or twice during the cooking time. Eat with your favorite sauce. Enjoy!

Nutrition:

Calories: 280   Carbohydrates: 5g

Fat: 14g   Protein: 14g

Fiber: 3g

126.   Easy Cheddar and Coriander Balls

Preparation time: 10 minutes   **Cooking time:** 20 minutes   **Servings:** 6

Ingredients:

- 1 cup almond flour
- ¼ cup flaxseed meal

- A pinch of salt
- ½ cup canola oil

- 1 cup cheddar cheese, cubed
- ½ cup green coriander, minced
- ¼ teaspoon cumin powder
- 1 teaspoon dried parsley flakes
- Water

Directions:
1. Firstly, make the dough by mixing the flour, salt, and canola oil; add water and knead it into dough. Let it stay for about 20 minutes.
2. Divide the dough into equal size balls. Sprinkle cheese cubes with green coriander, cumin powder, and parsley.
3. Now, press the cheese cubes down into the center of the dough balls. Then, pinch the edges securely to form a ball. Repeat with the rest of the dough.
4. Lay the balls in the Air Fryer's cooking basket; spritz each ball with a cooking spray, coating on all sides. After that, cook for 8 to 10 minutes, shaking the basket once during the cooking time.
5. Serve with your favorite sauce for dipping. Bon appétit!

Nutrition:

Calories: 150

Fat: 3g

Fiber: 2g

Carbohydrates: 7g

Protein: 10g

127. Nutmeg Okra

Preparation time: 10 minutes   **Cooking time:** 10 minutes   **Servings:** 4

Ingredients:
- 1-pound okra, trimmed
- 3 oz. pancetta, sliced
- ½ teaspoon ground nutmeg
- ½ teaspoon salt
- 1 teaspoon sunflower oil

Directions:
1. Sprinkle okra with ground nutmeg and salt. Then put the vegetables in the air fryer and sprinkle with sunflower. Chop pancetta roughly. Top the okra with pancetta and cook the meal for 10 minutes at 360F.

Nutrition:

Calories: 160

Fat: 2g

Fiber: 5g

Carbohydrates: 10g

Protein: 8g

128. Falafel with Homemade Mayonnaise

Preparation time: 10 minutes   **Cooking time:** 15 minutes   **Servings:** 2

Ingredients:

Falafel:
- ½ pound cauliflower
- ½ onion, chopped
- 2 cloves garlic, minced
- 2 tablespoons fresh cilantro leaves, chopped
- ¼ cup almond meal
- ½ teaspoon baking powder
- 1 teaspoon cumin powder
- A pinch of ground cardamom
- Sea salt and ground black pepper

Homemade Mayonnaise:
- 1 egg yolk
- 1 tablespoon sour cream
- ¼ cup olive oil
- ¼ teaspoon salt
- 1 tablespoon lemon juice

Directions:
1. Pulse all the falafel ingredients in your food processor.
2. Form the falafel mixture into balls and set them in the lightly greased Air Fryer basket.
3. Cook at 380F for about 15 minutes, shaking the basket occasionally to ensure even cooking.
4. In a mixing bowl, place egg yolk and sour cream. Gradually and slowly, pour in your oil while whisking constantly.
5. Once you reach a thick consistency, add in the salt and lemon juice. Whisk again to combine. Serve falafel with your homemade mayonnaise and enjoy!

Nutrition:

Calories: 38

Fat: 1.7g

Fiber: 2.3g

Carbohydrates: 4.5g

Protein: 1.8g

129. Feta Peppers

Preparation time: 10 minutes   **Cooking time:** 15 minutes   **Servings:** 4

Ingredients:

- 5 oz. Feta, crumbled
- 8 oz. banana pepper, trimmed
- 1 teaspoon sesame oil
- 1 garlic clove, minced
- ½ teaspoon fresh dill, chopped
- 1 teaspoon lemon juice
- ½ teaspoon lime zest, grated

Directions:

1. Clean the seeds from the peppers and cut them into halves. Then sprinkle the peppers with sesame oil and put in the air fryer. Cook them for 10 minutes at 385F. Flip the peppers on another side after 5 minutes of cooking. Meanwhile, mix up minced garlic, fresh dill, lemon juice, and lime zest. Put the cooked banana peppers on the plate and sprinkle with lemon juice mixture. Then top the vegetables with crumbled feta.

Nutrition:

Calories: 120   Carbohydrates: 8g

Fat: 1g   Protein: 15g

Fiber: 4g

130. Halloumi Skewers

Preparation time: 15 minutes   **Cooking time:** 14 minutes   **Servings:** 4

Ingredients:

- 10 oz. halloumi cheese
- 1 eggplant
- 1 green bell pepper
- 1 teaspoon dried cilantro
- 1 tablespoon avocado oil
- ½ teaspoon salt
- 1 teaspoon chili flakes

Directions:

1. Chop eggplant, pepper, and eggplant roughly. Then chop halloumi. Put all ingredients from the list above in the big bowl and shake well. Then string the ingredients on the wooden skewers and place in the air fryer.
2. Cook the kebabs for 14 minutes at 400F. Flip the kebabs on another side after 6 minutes of cooking.

Nutrition:

Calories: 87   Carbohydrates: 5.9g

Fat: 7.3g   Protein: 1.3g

Fiber: 2g

131. Hungarian Pilau with Mushrooms and Herbs

Preparation time: 10 minutes   **Cooking time:** 15 minutes   **Servings:** 4

Ingredients:

- 1 ½ cups cauliflower rice
- 3 cups vegetable broth
- 2 tablespoons olive oil
- 1 pound fresh porcini mushrooms, sliced
- 2 tablespoons olive oil
- 2 garlic cloves
- 1 onion, chopped
- ¼ cup dry vermouth
- 1 teaspoon dried thyme
- ½ teaspoon dried tarragon
- 1 teaspoon sweet Hungarian paprika

Directions:

1. Thoroughly combine cauliflower rice with the remaining ingredients in a lightly greased baking dish.
2. Cook in the preheated Air Fryer at 370for 20 minutes, checking periodically to ensure even cooking.
3. Serve in individual bowls. Bon appétit!

Nutrition:

Calories: 17   Carbohydrates: 7g

Fat: 4g   Protein: 12g

Fiber: 3g

132. Lime Olives and Zucchini

Preparation time: 5 minutes   **Cooking time:** 12 minutes   **Servings:** 4

Ingredients:

- 4 zucchinis, sliced
- 2cup kalamata olives, pitted
- Salt and black pepper to the taste
- 2 tablespoons lime juice
- ½ tablespoons olive oil
- 2 teaspoons balsamic vinegar

Directions:

1. In a pan, mix the olives with all the other ingredients, toss, introduce in the fryer and cook at 390F for 12 minutes. Divide the mix between plates and serve.

Nutrition:

Calories: 140

Fat: 1g

Fiber: 1g

Carbohydrates: 2g

Protein: 10g

133. Cream Cheese Green Beans

Preparation time: 15 minutes   **Cooking time:** 5 minutes   **Servings:** 2

Ingredients:

- 8 oz. green beans
- 1 egg, beaten
- 1 teaspoon cream cheese
- ¼ cup almond flour
- ¼ cup coconut flakes
- ½ teaspoon ground black pepper
- ½ teaspoon salt
- 1 teaspoon sesame oil

Directions:

1. In the mixing bowl mix up cream cheese, egg, and ground black pepper. Add salt. In the separated bowl mix up coconut flakes and almond flour.
2. Preheat the air fryer to 400F.S ink the green beans in the egg mixture and then coat in the coconut flakes mixture. Repeat the step one more time and transfer the vegetables in the air fryer. Sprinkle them with sesame oil and cook for 5 minutes. Shake the vegetables after 2 minutes of cooking if you don't put green beans in one layer.

Nutrition:

Calories: 123

Fat: 8g

Protein: 8g

Carbohydrates: 3g

Fiber: 1g

134. Cauli Rice Salad with Tomatoes

Preparation time: 10 minutes   **Cooking time:** 15 minutes   **Servings:** 4

Ingredients:

- 1 pound cauliflower rice
- 2 garlic cloves, pressed
- ⅓ cup coriander, chopped
- 1 cup shallots, chopped
- 4 ounces tomato, sliced
- 1 cup arugula lettuce, torn into pieces
- 2 tablespoons apple cider vinegar
- Sea salt and ground black pepper

Directions:

1. Put cauliflower rice into the Air Fryer basket. Cook at 375F for 10 minutes.
2. Transfer the prepared couscous to a nice salad bowl. Add the remaining ingredients; stir to combine and enjoy!
3. Bon appétit!

Nutrition:

Calories: 180

Fat: 4g

Fiber: 3g

Carbohydrates: 7g

Protein: 14g

135. Taco Okra

Preparation time: 10 minutes   **Cooking time:** 10 minutes   **Servings:** 2

Ingredients:

- 9 oz. okra, chopped
- 1 teaspoon taco seasoning
- 1 teaspoon sunflower oil

Directions:

1. In the mixing bowl mix up chopped okra, taco seasoning, and sunflower oil. Then preheat the air fryer to 385F. Put the okra mixture in the air fryer and cook it for 5 minutes. Then shake the vegetables well and cook them for 5 minutes more.

Nutrition:

Calories: 240
Fat: 14g
Fiber: 2g

Carbohydrates: 4g
Protein: 16g

136.   Smoked Tempeh

Preparation time: 10 minutes   **Cooking time:** 6 minutes   **Servings:** 2

Ingredients:

- 1 cup tempeh
- 1 teaspoon apple cider vinegar
- 1 teaspoon sesame oil

- ½ teaspoon garlic powder
- 1 teaspoon liquid smoke
- 1 teaspoon butter, melted

Directions:

1. In the shallow bowl mix up melted butter, liquid smoke, garlic powder, sesame oil, and apple cider vinegar. Cut the tempeh into halves and brush with apple cider vinegar mixture from both sides. After this, preheat the air fryer to 400F.
2. Put the tempeh in the air fryer and cook it for 3 minutes from each side or until it is light brown. Transfer the cooked tempeh to the serving plate. Vegan Reuben is cooked.

Nutrition:

Calories: 166
Protein: 4g
Fiber: 5g

Fat: 13g
Carbohydrates: 12g
Sugar: 4g

137.   Ghee Lemony Endives

Preparation time: 5 minutes   **Cooking time:** 15 minutes   **Servings:** 4

Ingredients:

- ½ tablespoons ghee, melted
- 12 endives, trimmed

- A pinch of salt and black pepper
- 1 tablespoon lemon juice

Directions:

1. In a bowl, mix the endives with the ghee, salt, pepper and lemon juice and toss. Put the endives in the fryer's basket and cook at 350F for 15 minutes.
2. Divide between plates and serve.

Nutrition:

Calories: 280
Fat: 14g
Fiber: 3g

Carbohydrates: 5g
Protein: 14g

138.   Coconut Kohlrabi Mash

Preparation time: 10 minutes   **Cooking time:** 20 minutes   **Servings:** 6

Ingredients:

- 12 oz. kohlrabi, chopped
- 2 tablespoons coconut cream
- 1 teaspoon salt

- ½ cup Monterey Jack cheese, shredded
- ¼ cup chicken broth
- ½ teaspoon chili flakes

Directions:

1. In the air fryer pan mix up kohlrabi, coconut cream, salt, Monterey jack cheese, chicken broth, and chili flakes. Then preheat the air fryer to 255F. Cook the meal for 20 minutes.

Nutrition:

Calories: 311
Fat: 6g

Carbohydrates: 12g
Proteins: 16g

139.   Herbed Kalamata Olives

Preparation time: 5 minutes   **Cooking time:** 8 minutes   **Servings:** 4

Ingredients:

- 8 Kalamata Olives, pitted

- 1 teaspoon Italian seasonings

- 1 tablespoon olive oil
- 1 teaspoon coconut aminos

Directions:
1. Sprinkle olives with Italian seasonings, olive oil, and coconut aminos.
2. Put the olives in the air fryer and cook at 360F for 8 minutes.

Nutrition:
Calories: 45

Carbohydrates: 0.9g

Fat: 4.8g

Protein: 0.1g

Fiber: 0.3g

140.   Cauliflower Balls

Preparation time: 15 minutes   **Cooking time:** 12 minutes   **Servings:** 4

Ingredients:
- 2 cups cauliflower, shredded
- 3 tablespoons coconut flour
- 1 teaspoon ground cumin
- 2 tablespoons coconut oil
- 1 egg, beaten
- 1 teaspoon salt
- 1 teaspoon ground coriander
- 1 teaspoon dried basil
- Cooking spray

Directions:
1. Mix shredded cauliflower with coconut flour, ground cumin, coconut oil, egg, salt, ground coriander, and dried basil.
2. Make the balls from the mixture and put it in the air fryer.
3. Spray the cauliflower balls with cooking spray and cook them at 385F for 6 minutes per side or until they are golden brown.

Nutrition:
Calories: 134

Carbohydrates: 9g

Fat: 9.6g

Protein: 4g

Fiber: 5.1g

Side Dishes

141. Kohlrabi Fries

Preparation time: 10 minutes　　**Cooking time:** 30 minutes　　**Servings:** 4

Ingredients:

- 2 pounds (907 g) kohlrabi, peeled and cut into ¼–½-inch fries
- 2 tablespoons olive oil
- Salt and freshly ground black pepper

Directions:

1. Preheat the air fryer to 400F (205C).
2. In a large bowl, merge the kohlrabi and olive oil. Season to taste with salt and black pepper. Toss gently until thoroughly coated.
3. Working in batches, if necessary, spread the kohlrabi in a single layer in the air fryer basket. Pausing halfway through the cooking time to shake the basket, air fry until the fries are lightly browned and crunchy.

Nutrition:

Calories: 120　　　　　　Carbohydrates: 14g

Fat: 7g　　　　　　Fiber: 2g

Protein: 4g

142. Pork Onion Rings

Preparation time: 10 minutes　　**Cooking time:** 5 minutes　　**Servings:** 8

Ingredients:

- 1 large egg
- ¼ cup coconut flour
- 2 ounces (57 g) plain pork rinds, finely crushed
- 1 large white onion

Directions:

1. Whisk egg in a medium bowl. Place coconut flour and pork rinds in two separate medium bowls. Dip each onion ring into egg, then coat in coconut flour. Dip coated onion ring in egg once more, then press gently into pork rinds to cover all sides.
2. Place rings into ungreased air fryer basket. Adjust the temperature to 400F (205C) and set the timer for 5 minutes, turning the onion rings halfway through cooking. Onion rings will be golden and crispy when done. Serve warm.

Nutrition:

Calories: 140　　　　　　Carbohydrates: 2g

Fat: 1g　　　　　　Protein: 10g

Fiber: 1g

143. Roasted Eggplant

Preparation time: 15 minutes　　**Cooking time:** 15 minutes　　**Servings:** 4

Ingredients:

- 1 large eggplant
- 2 tablespoons olive oil
- ¼ teaspoon salt
- ½ teaspoon garlic powder

Directions:

1. Remove top and bottom from eggplant. Slice eggplant into ¼-inch-thick round slices.
2. Brush slices with olive oil. Sprinkle with salt and garlic powder. Set eggplant slices into the air fryer basket.
3. Adjust the temperature to 390F (199C) and set the timer for 15 minutes.
4. Serve immediately.

Nutrition:

Calories: 236　　　　　　Carbohydrates: 5g

Fat: 13g　　　　　　Fiber: 0g

Protein: 19g

144. Roasted Salsa

Preparation time: 5 minutes　　**Cooking time:** 30 minutes　　**Servings:** 2

Ingredients:

- 2 large San Marzano tomatoes, cored and cut into large chunks
- ½ medium white onion, peeled and large-diced
- ½ medium jalapeño, seeded and large-diced
- 2 cloves garlic, peeled and diced
- ½ teaspoon salt
- 1 tablespoon coconut oil
- ¼ cup fresh lime juice

Directions:
1. Place tomatoes, onion, and jalapeño into an ungreased 6-inch round nonstick baking dish. Add garlic, then sprinkle with salt and drizzle with coconut oil.
2. Place dish into air fryer basket. Adjust the temperature to 300F (150C) and set the timer for 30 minutes. Vegetables will be dark brown around the edges and tender when done.
3. Pour mixture into a food processor or blender. Add lime juice. Process on low speed 30 seconds until only a few chunks remain.
4. Transfer salsa to a sealable container and refrigerate at least 1 hour. Serve chilled.

Nutrition:
Calories: 28
Fat: 2g
Protein: 1g

Carbohydrates: 3g
Fiber: 1g

145. Sausage-Stuffed Mushroom Caps
Preparation time: 10 minutes **Cooking time:** 8 minutes **Servings:** 2
Ingredients:
- 6 large portobello mushroom caps
- ½ pound (227g) Italian sausage
- ¼ cup chopped onion
- 2 tablespoons blanched finely ground almond flour
- ¼ cup grated Parmesan cheese
- 1 teaspoon minced fresh garlic

Directions:
1. Use a spoon to set out each mushroom cap, reserving scrapings.
2. In a skillet over medium heat, brown the sausage about 10 minutes or until fully cooked and no pink remains. Drain and then add reserved mushroom scrapings, onion, almond flour, Parmesan, and garlic. Gently bend ingredients together and continue cooking an additional minute, then remove from heat.
3. Evenly scoop the mixture into mushroom caps and place the caps into a 6-inch round pan. Place pan into the air fryer basket.
4. Adjust the temperature to 375F (190C) and set the timer for 8 minutes.
5. When done cooking, the tops will be browned and bubbling. Serve warm.

Nutrition:
Calories: 261
Fat: 8g

Carbohydrates: 19g
Proteins: 16g

146. Tomato Salad with Arugula
Preparation time: 10 minutes **Cooking time:** 10 minutes **Servings:** 4
Ingredients:
- 4 green tomatoes
- ½ teaspoon salt
- 1 large egg, lightly beaten
Buttermilk Dressing:
- 1 cup mayonnaise
- ½ cup sour cream
- 2 teaspoons fresh lemon juice
- 2 tablespoons finely chopped fresh parsley
- 1 teaspoon dried dill
- ½ cup almond flour
- 1 tablespoon Creole seasoning
- 1 (5 ounce / 142-g) bag arugula

- 1 teaspoon dried chives
- ½ teaspoon salt
- ½ teaspoon garlic powder
- ½ teaspoon onion powder

Directions:
1. Preheat the air fryer to 400F (205C).
2. Set the tomatoes into ½-inch slices and sprinkle with the salt. Let sit for 5 to 10 minutes.

3. Set the egg in a small shallow bowl. In another small shallow bowl, combine the almond flour and Creole seasoning. Sink each tomato slice into the egg wash, then dip into the almond flour mixture, turning to coat evenly.
4. Working in batches, if necessary, arrange the tomato slices in a single layer in the air fryer basket and spray both sides lightly with olive oil. Air fry until browned and crisp, 8 to 10 minutes.
5. To make the buttermilk dressing: In a small bowl, whisk together the mayonnaise, sour cream, lemon juice, parsley, dill, chives, salt, garlic powder, and onion powder.
6. Serve the tomato slices on top of a bed of the arugula with the dressing on the side.

Nutrition:

Calories: 281

Fat: 3g

Carbohydrates: 10g

Proteins: 14g

147.   Tomato and Zucchini Boats

Preparation time: 5 minutes   **Cooking time:** 10 minutes   **Servings:** 4

Ingredients:

- 1 large zucchini, ends removed, halved lengthwise
- 6 grape tomatoes, quartered
- ¼ teaspoon salt
- ¼ cup feta cheese
- 1 tablespoon balsamic vinegar
- 1 tablespoon olive oil

Directions:

1. Use a spoon to scoop out 2 tablespoons from center of each zucchini half, making just enough space to fill with tomatoes and feta.
2. Place tomatoes evenly in centers of zucchini halves and sprinkle with salt. Place into ungreased air fryer basket. Adjust the temperature to 350F (180C) and set the timer for 10 minutes. When done, zucchini will be tender.
3. Transfer boats to a serving tray and sprinkle with feta, then drizzle with vinegar and olive oil. Serve warm.

Nutrition:

Calories: 142

Fat: 3g

Fiber: 2g

Carbohydrates: 6g

Protein: 4g

148.   Potato Spud

Preparation time: 8 minutes   **Cooking time:** 20-25 minutes   **Servings:** 2

Ingredients:

- 1 spoonful of olive oil
- 1 spoonful of sweet chili sauce
- 1½ spoonful of sour cream
- 1 potato, cut into wedges
- black pepper and salt to improve the flavor

Directions:

1. Toss potato wedges with oil, Salt, and pepper in a mixing bowl, then transfer to an air fryer basket and cook for about 25 minutes, flipping once.
2. Serve potato wedges as a side dish with sour cream and chili sauce drizzled all over them.

Nutrition:

Calories: 187

Fat: 3g

Fiber: 0.2g

Carbohydrates: 3.2g

Protein: 34.7g

149.   Baked Mushroom

Preparation time: 5 minutes   **Cooking time:** 10 minutes   **Servings:** 2

Ingredients:

- 1 spoonful of grated mozzarella
- 1 spoonful of grated cheddar cheese
- ½ spoonful of chopped dill
- 5 buttons of stem removed from mushrooms
- ½ spoonful of olive oil
- ½ spoonful of Italian seasoning
- Salt and black pepper to taste

Directions:

1. Combine mushrooms, Italian seasoning, Salt, pepper, oil, and dill in a bowl and rub well.

2. Place the mushrooms inside the air fryer basket, top with mozzarella and cheddar, and cook for 8 minutes at 360F.
3. Serve them as a side dish by dividing among plates.

Nutrition:

Calories: 221

Fat: 12g

Fiber: 2g

Carbohydrates: 5g

Protein: 14g

150.   Chipped Potatoes

Preparation time: 9 minutes   **Cooking time:** 20 minutes   **Servings:** 2

Ingredients:

- A small quantity of ginger powder
- 2 spoonful's of olive oil
- ½ spoon of grounded cumin
- ¼ cup of ketchup
- A little cinnamon powder
- A pinch of cinnamon powder
- ½ spoon of curry powder
- ¼ spoon of grounded coriander
- 2 sweet potatoes
- 2 spoonful's of mayonnaise
- Salt and black pepper to taste

Directions:

1. Merge sweet potato fries with Salt, pepper, coriander, curry powder, and oil in the basket of your air fryer, toss well, and cook at 370F for 20 minutes, flipping once.
2. Meanwhile, whisk together the ketchup, mayonnaise, cumin, ginger, and cinnamon in a mixing bowl.
3. Serve as a side dish by placing fries on plates and drizzling ketchup mixture over them.

Nutrition:

Calories: 243

Protein: 6g

Fiber: 3g

Fat: 20g

Sodium: 647mg

Carbohydrates: 12g

151.   Corncob with Cheese

Preparation time: 8 minutes   **Cooking time:** 16 minutes   **Servings:** 1

Ingredients:

- ½ cup of grated feta cheese
- 2 spoons of sweet paprika
- Juice extracted from two limes
- 2 corns on the cob with the husks removed
- A drizzle of olive oil

Directions:

1. Corn should be rubbed with oil and paprika, placed in an air fryer, and cooked for 15 minutes at 400F, flipping once.
2. Serve as a side dish by placing corn on plates, sprinkling cheese on top, and drizzled with lime juice.

Nutrition:

Calories: 314

Fat: 16.8g

Fiber: 3.4g

Carbohydrates: 7.5g

Protein: 33.9g

152.   Baked Potatoes

Preparation time: 10 minutes   **Cooking time:** 20 minutes   **Servings:** 2

Ingredients:

- ½ spoon of dried basil
- ½ spoon of sweet paprika
- 2 spoonful's of olive oil
- ½ spoon of dried oregano
- 1 spoon of minced garlic
- 2 peeled and thinly sliced potatoes
- Salt and black pepper to taste

Directions:

1. Whisk together the oil, garlic, Salt, pepper, oregano, basil, and paprika, in a mixing cup.
2. Rub the potatoes with this mixture, put them in the basket of your air fryer and cook for approximately 20 minutes at 360F.
3. Serve as a side dish by dividing them among plates.

Nutrition:

Calories: 136

Fat: 9.3g

Carbohydrates: 2.1g

Protein: 11.4g

153.　　　Corn Bread

Preparation time: 10 minutes　　　**Cooking time:** 15 minutes　　　**Servings:** 3

Ingredients:

- ½ spoon of chopped thyme
- 1 spoon of minced garlic ice
- 1½ cups of vegan breadcrumbs
- ¼ cup of coconut cream
- 1 cup of coconut milk
- ½ chopped yellow onion
- 1 spoonful of olive oil
- ¼ cup of chopped celery
- 1 cup of corn
- ¼ cup of chopped red bell pepper
- Salt and black pepper to taste

Directions:

1. Heat the oil in a pan over minimal-high heat, then add the corn, celery, onion, bell pepper, Salt, pepper, garlic, and thyme, mix to combine, and cook for 10 minutes before transferring to an air fryer-safe pan.
2. Stir in the coconut milk and cocoa cream.
3. Place the corn mixture in your air fryer, top with breadcrumbs, and cook for 40 minutes at 320F.
4. Serve as a side dish by dividing the mixture between dishes.

Nutrition:

Calories: 236　　　　　　　　　　　　Carbohydrates: 5g
Fat: 13g　　　　　　　　　　　　　　Fiber: 0g
Protein: 19g

154.　　　Spiced Broccoli

Preparation time: 10 minutes　　　**Cooking time:** 15 minutes　　　**Servings:** 4

Ingredients:

- 2 chopped shallots
- 2 spoonful's of horseradish
- ¼ spoon of grounded nutmeg
- 1½ pounds of halved Brussels sprouts
- ½ spoon of chopped thyme
- A drizzle of olive oil
- 2 spoonful's of almond flour
- ½ spoon of coconut cream
- Salt and black pepper to taste

Directions:

1. Toss sprouts in a bowl with a drizzle of oil, Salt, and pepper to cover. Cook at 400 degrees F for 20 minutes in your air fryer, then move to a plan that suits your free plans.
2. Then add shallots, flour, coconut cream, nutmeg, and thyme. Place the pan in the fryer and cook for another 10 minutes at 400F.
3. As a side dish, you will divide the sprouts mixture between sprout top with horseradish and serve.

Nutrition:

Calories: 140　　　　　　　　　　　　Carbohydrates: 2g
Fat: 1g　　　　　　　　　　　　　　Protein: 10g
Fiber: 1g

155.　　　Cauliflower Patties

Preparation time: 10 minutes　　　**Cooking time:** 9 minutes　　　**Servings:** 2

Ingredients:

- 3 oz. puff pastry
- 7 oz. mashed cauliflower
- 1 egg yolk
- ½ teaspoon cumin
- ¼ teaspoon salt
- 1 oz. carrot, sautéed

Directions:

1. Set the puff pastry and cut it into the triangles. Then combine the sautéed carrot with the mashed cauliflower. Place the filing on the triangles and secure them well.
2. Whisk the egg and brush the patties. Sprinkle the patties with the cumin and salt.
3. Preheat the air fryer to 390F.
4. Put the patties on the air fryer rack and cook for 9 minutes. When the patties are golden brown, they are cooked. Transfer them to the serving plates.
5. Enjoy!

Nutrition:

Calories: 92

Fat: 2.1g

Carbohydrates: 13.9g

Protein 5.9g

156.   Parmesan Mushrooms

Preparation time: 10 minutes   **Cooking time:** 6 minutes   **Servings:** 2

Ingredients:

- 3 oz. parmesan, shredded
- 3 oz. cottage cheese
- 2 tablespoon fresh parsley, chopped
- ¼ teaspoon minced garlic
- ½ teaspoon butter
- 2 Portobello mushroom hats
- ⅓ teaspoon salt

Directions:

1. Peel the mushroom hats. Combine chopped parsley, minced garlic, cottage cheese, salt, and butter. Mix it with the help of the hand blender.
2. Preheat the air fryer to 400F.
3. Fill the mushrooms with the cottage cheese mixture and put them in the air fryer basket.
4. Cook the mushrooms for 4 minutes. Then sprinkle the mushrooms with the shredded cheese and cook for 2 minutes more. Let the cooked mushrooms chill gently.
5. Serve the meal!

Nutrition:

Calories: 120

Fat: 3.9g

Carbohydrates 1.9g

Protein: 1.9g

157.   Baby Carrots with Greens

Preparation time: 7 minutes   **Cooking time:** 12 minutes   **Servings:** 2

Ingredients:

- 1 cup baby carrot
- ½ teaspoon salt
- ½ teaspoon white pepper
- 1 tablespoon honey
- 1 teaspoon sesame oil

Directions:

1. Preheat the air fryer to 385F.
2. Combine the baby carrot with the salt, white pepper, and sesame oil. Shake the baby carrot and transfer in the air fryer basket. Cook the vegetables for 10 minutes.
3. After this, add honey and shake the vegetables.
4. Cook the meal for 2 minutes. After this, shake the vegetables and serve immediately.
5. Enjoy!

Nutrition:

Calories: 192

Fat: 16.4g

Fiber: 2g

Carbohydrates: 4.8g

Protein: 7.7g

158.   Smashed Red Potatoes

Preparation time: 15 minutes   **Cooking time:** 15 minutes   **Servings:** 2

Ingredients:

- 4 red potatoes
- ¼ cup cream cheese
- ½ tablespoon onion powder
- 4 tablespoon chicken stock
- ½ teaspoon salt
- 1 tablespoon butter
- ½ teaspoon olive oil

Directions:

1. Wash the potatoes and peel them. Chop the potatoes roughly and sprinkle with the olive oil and salt.
2. Preheat the air fryer to 400F.
3. Set the potato in the air fryer basket and add butter. Cook the potato for 10 minutes.
4. Shake the potato after 7 minutes of cooking. After this, smash the potatoes with the help of the fork.
5. Add onion powder, chicken stock, and cream cheese. Mix the potatoes until homogenous and serve.
6. Taste it!

Nutrition:

Calories: 38

Fat: 1.7g

Fiber: 2.3g

Carbohydrates: 4.5g

Protein: 1.8 g

159. Garlic Vegetable Chunks

Preparation time: 10 minutes   **Cooking time:** 15 minutes   **Servings:** 2

Ingredients:

- 1 zucchini
- 1 red sweet pepper
- 1 teaspoon garlic powder
- 2 tablespoon olive oil
- 2 tablespoon soy sauce
- 1 teaspoon lemon zest
- 1 teaspoon minced garlic
- ¼ teaspoon cumin
- ½ teaspoon salt

Directions:

1. Preheat the air fryer to 400F.
2. Remove the seeds from the sweet pepper. Cut the zucchini and sweet pepper into 1-inch chunks.
3. Put the vegetables into separate bowls. Sprinkle the vegetables with the soy sauce, lemon zest, minced garlic, cumin, and salt. Put the peppers into the air fryer basket and cook for 3 minutes.
4. Then add zucchini and shake the meal. Sprinkle it with the olive oil and cook for 11 minutes more. Shake the vegetables after 4 minutes of cooking.
5. When the vegetables are tender – they are cooked.
6. Serve the meal only hot.

Nutrition:

Calories: 81

Protein: 0.4g

Carbs: 4.7g

Fat: 8.3g

160. Danish Cinnamon Rolls

Preparation time: 5minutes   **Cooking time:** 20 minutes   Serving: 4

Ingredients:

- 9 ounces refrigerated crescent rolls
- 1 tablespoon coconut oil
- 4 tablespoons stevia
- 1 teaspoon ground cinnamon

Directions:

1. Separate the dough into rectangles. Mix the remaining ingredients until well combined.
2. Spread each rectangle with the cinnamon mixture; roll them up tightly.
3. Place the rolls in the Air Fryer cooking basket.
4. Bake the rolls at 300 F for about 5 minutes; turn them over and bake for a further 5 minutes.
5. Bon appétit!

Nutrition:

Calories: 422

Protein: 11g

Fiber: 11g

Carbohydrates: 12g

Fat: 37g

Snacks and Appetizer

161.   Brussels Sprout Chips

Preparation time: 14 minutes   **Cooking time:** 15 minutes   **Servings:** 6

Ingredients:

- 1 lb. Brussels sprout slices
- Avocado oil or olive oil
- Salt, to taste
- Pepper, to taste
- Garlic powder, to taste
- Onion powder, to taste

Directions:

1. Toss the washed Brussels sprout slices with oil, salt, pepper, onion powder, and garlic powder.
2. Spread these slices in the Air Fryer basket and return the basket to the fryer.
3. Air fry them for 5 minutes at 370 degrees F then toss them well.
4. Air fry the slices again for 5 more minutes.
5. Adjust seasoning with more spices and cooking oil.
6. Air fry these slices again for 5 minutes then toss them.
7. Cook for another 3 minutes.
8. Serve them.

Nutrition:

Calories: 242

Fat: 15g

Carbohydrates: 4.8g

Protein: 6g

162.   Zucchini Carrot Fries

Preparation time: 14 minutes   **Cooking time:** 10 minutes   **Servings:** 6

Ingredients:

- 1 medium zucchini, spiralized
- 1 medium carrot, spiralized
- 1 large egg, beaten
- ½ cup almond flour
- ½ cup parmesan cheese, grated
- 1 teaspoon Italian seasoning
- ½ teaspoons garlic powder
- Pinch of salt and black pepper
- Oil for spraying

Directions:

1. Mix almond flour with parmesan and all the spices in a shallow bowl.
2. Dip the zucchini and carrots spirals first in the egg, then dredge them through the flour mixture.
3. Spread the coated zucchini and carrots in the Air Fryer basket and return the basket to the fryer.
4. Cook for 10 minutes at 400F until crispy. Serve warm.

Nutrition:

Calories: 292

Fat: 16.3g

Carbohydrates: 7.9g

Protein: 29g

163.   Blooming Onion

Preparation time: 14 minutes   **Cooking time:** 10 minutes   **Servings:** 6

Ingredients:

- 1 large onion
- 2 ½ cups almond flour
- 4 teaspoons Old Bay seasoning
- 2 eggs, beaten
- ½ cup coconut milk

Directions:

1. Slice the top of the onion while keeping its base intact.
2. Wash it well and drain all the water out of it.
3. Carve several slits vertically from top to bottom at equal distances. Make sure to keep the cut up to one inch above the base.
4. Spread the onion layers like flower petals and set them aside.
5. Preheat the Air Fryer to 400F.
6. Whisk eggs with the milk in one bowl and mix flour with seasoning in another.
7. Dust the onion flower with flour mixture, then dip it in the egg mixture.

8. Sprinkle the remaining flour mixture over it and shake off the excess.
9. Place the onion flower in the Air Fryer basket and return the basket to the fryer.
10. Air fry the onion for 10 minutes in the preheated Air Fryer. Serve.

Nutrition:

Calories: 283

Carbohydrates: 8.1g

Fat: 17.1g

Protein: 6g

164. Chicken Pops

Preparation time: 14 minutes   **Cooking time:** 8 minutes   **Servings:** 6

Ingredients:

Marinade:

- 2 lbs. chicken breast tenders, diced
- 2 cups almond milk
- 1 teaspoon salt

- ½ teaspoons black pepper
- ½ teaspoons ground paprika

Dry **Ingredients:**

- 3 cups almond flour
- 3 teaspoons salt
- 2 teaspoons black pepper

- 2 teaspoons paprika
- Oil spray

Directions:

1. Attach all the ingredients for the marinade in a Ziploc bag.
2. Place the chicken in it then zip the bag. Shake it well then refrigerate for 2 hours or more.
3. Meanwhile, mix all the dry ingredients in a shallow container.
4. Detach the chicken from the marinade and dredge the pieces through the dry mixture.
5. Shake off the excess then place the pieces in the Air Fryer basket.
6. Spray them with cooking oil then return the basket to the Air Fryer.
7. Air Fry them for 8 minutes at 370 degrees and toss them when cooked halfway through. Serve immediately.

Nutrition:

Calories: 296

Carbohydrates: 7g

Fat: 16g

Protein: 6g

165. Breaded Mushrooms

Preparation time: 14 minutes   **Cooking time:** 7 minutes   **Servings:** 6

Ingredients:

- ½ lb. button mushrooms
- 1 cup almond flour
- 1 egg

- 1 cup almond meal
- 3 oz. grated Parmigianino Reggiano cheese
- Salt and black pepper, to taste, to taste

Directions:

1. Let your Air Fryer preheat to 360F.
2. Toss almond meal with cheese in a shallow bowl. Whisk egg in one bowl and spread flour in another.
3. Wash mushrooms then pat dry. Coat each mushroom with flour. Dip each of them in the egg then finally in the almond meal mixture. Shake off the excess and place the mushrooms in the Air Fryer basket.
4. Spray them with cooking oil and return the basket to the fryer. Air fry these mushrooms for 7 minutes in the preheated Air Fryer.
5. Toss the mushrooms once cooked halfway through then continue cooking. Serve warm.

Nutrition:

Calories: 279

Carbohydrates: 8.3 g

Fat: 14.9g

Protein: 6g

166. Monkey Bread

Preparation time: 14 minutes   **Cooking time:** 7 minutes   **Servings:** 6

Ingredients:

- 1 cup almond flour
- 1 cup non-fat Greek yogurt

- 1 teaspoon Erythritol
- ½ teaspoons cinnamon

Directions:

1. Combine yogurt with flour to create a smooth dough in a mixing bowl.

2. Set the dough into 8 equal pieces and roll them into small balls.
3. Merge cinnamon with Swerve Erythritol in a shallow bowl.
4. Roll each ball in the cinnamon mixture and coat well.
5. Place these balls in the Air Fryer basket and return the basket to the fryer basket.
6. Cook these bread balls for 7 minutes at 375F on Air Fry Mode. Serve.

Nutrition:

Calories: 269	Carbohydrates: 4.8g
Fat: 16.3g	Protein: 18g

167.   Cheesecake Bites

Preparation time: 14 minutes   **Cooking time:** 2 minutes   **Servings:** 6

Ingredients:
- 8 oz. cream cheese, softened
- ½ cup Erythritol
- 4 tablespoons heavy cream
- ½ teaspoons vanilla extract
- ½ cup almond flour
- 2 tablespoons Erythritol

Directions:
1. Beat cream cheese with vanilla, ½ cup Erythritol and 2 tablespoons heavy cream in an electric mixer.
2. Scoop out batter into individual balls and place them on a 7-quart baking pan lined with parchment paper.
3. Freeze these balls for 30 minutes.
4. Meanwhile, whisk almond flour with 2 tablespoons Erythritol in a shallow bowl.
5. Dip the frozen balls in the remaining heavy cream then roll them in the flour mixture.
6. Arrange these coated balls in the Air Fryer basket then return the basket to the fryer.
7. Cook them for 2 minutes at 350F on Air Fry Mode. Allow them to cool then serve.

Nutrition:

Calories: 281	Carbohydrates: 9g
Fat: 20g	Protein: 10g

168.   Eggplant with Bacon

Preparation time: 14 minutes   **Cooking time:** 35 minutes   **Servings:** 6

Ingredients:
- 2 eggplants, cut in half lengthwise
- ½ cup shredded cheddar cheese
- 2 teaspoons salt
- 2 tablespoons cooked bacon bits
- 2 tablespoons sour cream
- Fresh scallions, sliced

Directions:
1. Place the crisper plate in the basket, then place the eggplants with their skin side down.
2. Return the basket to the Air Fryer. Select Air Fry mode for 35 minutes at 390 degrees F.
3. Once done, remove eggplants from the basket.
4. Top each half with chili and cheese.
5. Place them back in the basket.
6. Cook them again for 3 minutes at the same mode and temperature.
7. Garnish with sour cream, scallions and bacon bits. Serve warm.

Nutrition:

Calories: 390	Carbohydrates: 6.2g
Fat: 17.1g	Protein: 29g

169.   Bacon Wrapped Poppers

Preparation time: 14 minutes   **Cooking time:** 15 minutes   **Servings:** 6

Ingredients:
- 12 bacon strips, cut in half

Dough:
- ⅔ cup water
- 3 tablespoons butter
- 1 tablespoon bacon fat
- 1 teaspoon salt
- ⅔ cup almond flour
- 2 eggs
- 2 oz. shredded extra-sharp white Cheddar cheese
- ½ cup diced jalapeno peppers
- 1 pinch cayenne pepper

- 1 pinch black pepper

Directions:
1. Preheat the Air Fryer with its basket at 400F for 3 minutes.
2. Combine butter with salt and water in a skillet on medium heat. Stir in flour and stir cook for 3 minutes. Transfer it to the bowl and mix with eggs and the remaining ingredients.
3. Wrap this dough in plastic wrap and refrigerate for 30 minutes. Now make small popper balls out of this dough.
4. Wrap a bacon piece around each ball. Place these balls in the basket without overstuffing the basket.
5. Select Air Fry mode for 15 minutes at 390 degrees.
6. Press Start/Pause button after 7 minutes, then flip the poppers. Resume cooking until it is done. Serve warm.

Nutrition:
Calories: 271

Carbohydrates: 6.9g

Fat: 16.3g

Protein: 6g

170. Tofu Stuffed Jalapeno

Preparation time: 14 minutes   **Cooking time:** 1- minutes   **Servings:** 6

Ingredients:
- 1 lb. crumbled tofu
- 1 (8 oz.) package cream cheese, softened
- 1 cup shredded Parmesan cheese
- 1 lb. large fresh jalapeno peppers halved lengthwise and seeded
- 1 (8 oz.) bottle Ranch dressing

Directions:
1. Combine tofu, cream cheese and ranch dressing in a bowl.
2. Slice the jalapeno in half, remove the seeds and clean it from inside.
3. Stuff the sliced jalapeno pieces with the pork mixture.
4. Set the peppers in the Air Fryer basket over its crisper plate with their skin side down.
5. Insert the basket in the fryer and select Air fry mode for 10 minutes at 350F.
6. Once done, serve warm.

Nutrition:
Calories: 284

Carbohydrates: 7g

Fat: 18g

Protein: 6g

171. Avocado Gratin

Preparation time: 14 minutes   **Cooking time:** 6 minutes   **Servings:** 6

Ingredients:
- 2 avocados, peeled and pitted
- 1 tablespoon parsley, chopped
- 2 tablespoons almond meal
- 4 tablespoons Parmesan cheese, grated
- 1 tablespoon vegetable oil
- pepper and salt to taste

Directions:
1. Warmth the Air Fryer for 3 minutes at 300F.
2. Slice the avocados lengthwise to get 8 equal-sized pieces.
3. Arrange these pieces in the Air Fryer basket with their skin side down.
4. Top each piece with parsley, almond meal, cheese, oil, salt, and pepper.
5. Return the basket to the fryer and select Air fry mode for 6 minutes at 360 degrees F.
6. Once done, serve warm with sauce.

Nutrition:
Calories: 242

Carbohydrates: 8g

Fat: 16.3g

Protein: 6g

172. Flaxseed Chips

Preparation time: 14 minutes   **Cooking time:** 20 minutes   **Servings:** 6

Ingredients:
- ¾ cups almond flour
- 1 ¾ cups mozzarella cheese, shredded
- 2 tablespoons salted butter, melted
- 1 large egg
- 2 tablespoons cream
- ½ teaspoons onion powder
- ½ teaspoons garlic powder
- ½ teaspoons mustard powder
- ½ teaspoons salt

Directions:
1. At 400F, preheat your Air Fryer.
2. Mix cheese, flour and the rest of the ingredients to make a dough.
3. Roll out this dough into a ¼ inch thick sheet.
4. Cut the dough into small triangles.
5. Place the dough triangles in the Air Fryer basket in batches.
6. Air fry them for 10-20 minutes until crispy and golden.
7. Serve.

Nutrition:
Calories: 269

Carbohydrates: 5.9g

Fat: 17.1g

Protein: 29g

173.   Seeds Crisp

Preparation time: 14 minutes   **Cooking time:** 20 minutes   **Servings:** 6

Ingredients:
- 1 ¾ cups mozzarella cheese, shredded
- 2 tablespoons butter, melted
- 1 large egg
- ¾ cups mixed nuts and seeds, chopped
- ½ teaspoons onion powder
- ½ teaspoons garlic powder
- ½ teaspoons mustard powder
- ½ teaspoons salt

Directions:
1. At 350F, preheat your Air Fryer.
2. Mix nuts, cheese and the rest of the ingredients to make a mixture.
3. Press this seeds mixture in a 7-quart baking pan.
4. Place this pan in the Air Fryer basket in batches.
5. Air fry them for 20 minutes until crispy and golden.
6. Break into pieces. Serve.

Nutrition:
Calories: 296

Carbohydrates: 7g

Fat: 17.4g

Protein: 18g

174.   Jalapeno Cheese Crisps

Preparation time: 14 minutes   **Cooking time:** 5 minutes   **Servings:** 6

Ingredients:
- 1 cup cheddar cheese, shredded
- 4 jalapeno peppers, sliced and deseeded
- Salt, to taste
- Black pepper, to taste

Directions:
1. At 350F, preheat your Air Fryer.
2. Toss cheese with spices in a bowl. Layer an Air Fryer basket with parchment paper.
3. Divide the cheese on the parchment paper into 1 tablespoon mounds while leaving 1-inch gap. Place one jalapeno slice on top of each cheese mound.
4. Press them a little to adjust.
5. Air fry them for 5 minutes and transfer the shrimp to a plate.
6. Cook more cheese crisps in the same way. Serve.

Nutrition:
Calories: 283

Carbohydrates: 4.8g

Fat: 13.8g

Protein: 10g

175.   Cheese Bombs

Preparation time: 14 minutes   **Cooking time:** 10 minutes   **Servings:** 6

Ingredients:
- 1 ¾ cups mozzarella cheese, shredded
- 2 tablespoons salted butter, melted
- 1 large egg
- 2 tablespoons sour cream
- ¾ cups blanched almond flour
- ½ teaspoons onion powder
- ½ teaspoons garlic powder
- ½ teaspoons mustard powder
- ½ teaspoons salt

Directions:

1. At 400F, preheat your Air Fryer.
2. Mix cheese, flour and the rest of the ingredients to make a dough.
3. Divide this mixture into 1-inch balls.
4. Set the balls in the Air Fryer basket in batches.
5. Air fry them for 10 minutes until crispy and golden.
6. Serve.

Nutrition:

Calories: 292   Carbohydrates: 8.1g

Fat: 16.3g   Protein: 6g

176.   Cheese Crisps

Preparation time: 14 minutes   **Cooking time:** 5 minutes   **Servings:** 4

Ingredients:

- 1 cup cheddar cheese, shredded
- Salt, to taste
- Black pepper, to taste

Directions:

1. At 350F, preheat your Air Fryer.
2. Toss cheese with spices in a bowl. Layer an Air Fryer basket with parchment paper.
3. Divide the cheese on the parchment paper into 1 tablespoon mounds while leaving 1-inch gap.
4. Air fry them for 5 minutes and transfer the shrimp to a plate.
5. Cook more cheese crisps in the same way. Serve.

Nutrition:

Calories: 390   Carbohydrates: 6.9g

Fat: 17.1g   Protein: 6g

177.   Olives Fritters

Preparation time: 5 minutes   **Cooking time:** 12 minutes   **Servings:** 6

Ingredients:

- Cooking spray
- ½ cup parsley
- 1 egg
- ½ cup almond flour
- Salt and black pepper
- 3 spring onions
- ½ cup kalamata olives, pitted and minced
- 3 zucchinis, grated

Directions:

1. In a bowl, merge all the ingredients except the cooking spray, stir well and shape medium fritters out of this mixture.
2. Place the fritters in your air fryer's basket, grease them with cooking spray and cook at 380F for 6 minutes on each side. Serve them as an appetizer

Nutrition:

Calories: 395   Carbohydrates: 5.7g

Fat: 15g   Protein: 6g

178.   Zucchini Poppers

Preparation time: 14 minutes   **Cooking time:** 10 minutes   **Servings:** 6

Ingredients:

- 4 zucchinis, cut into cubes
- 1 teaspoon ground turmeric
- 8 tablespoons almond flour
- 2 teaspoons red chili powder
- 8 tablespoons plain yogurt
- 1 teaspoon ground cumin
- Salt, to taste

Directions:

1. In a bowl, add yogurt, spices and zucchini cubes. Mix well. Coat the zucchini cubes with almond flour.
2. Meanwhile, preheat the Air Fryer to 395F.
3. Place zucchini poppers in the Air Fryer basket and cook for about 10 minutes. Take out and serve.

Nutrition:

Calories: 271	Carbohydrates: 7g
Fat: 14.9g	Protein: 6g

179. Tuna Croquettes

Preparation time: 14 minutes　　**Cooking time:** 7 minutes　　**Servings:** 4

Ingredients:

- 14 oz. canned tuna, drained
- 2 tablespoons fresh parsley, chopped
- ½ cup vegetable oil
- 1 cup almond meal
- 2 eggs, beaten
- Salt and black pepper, to taste

Directions:

1. Add tuna to a bowl and mash well.
2. Then, add parsley, egg, salt and black pepper, to taste. Mix well.
3. Make equal-sized croquettes from the mixture.
4. Take a shallow dish and mix oil and almond meal in it.
5. Meanwhile, preheat the Air Fryer to 385F.
6. Place croquettes in the almond meal mixture and coat well. Set them in the Air Fryer basket and cook for about 7 minutes.
7. Take out and serve hot.

Nutrition:

Calories: 269	Carbohydrates: 7.9g
Fat: 16.3g	Protein: 6g

180. Salmon Nuggets

Preparation time: 14 minutes　　**Cooking time:** 10 minutes　　**Servings:** 6

Ingredients:

- 2 tablespoons olive oil
- 1-pound salmon, boneless and cubed
- 1 cup almond flour
- 2 eggs
- ½ cup almond meal
- Salt, to taste

Directions:

1. Take three shallow dishes.
2. Place flour in first, beaten eggs in second and almond meal, oil and salt in the third.
3. Now, coat cod strips in flour, dip in beaten eggs and roll into the bread-crumbs mixture.
4. Meanwhile, preheat the Air Fryer to 385 degrees F.
5. Arrange nuggets in the Air Fryer basket and cook for about 10 minutes. Take out and serve hot.

Nutrition:

Calories: 296	Carbohydrates: 9g
Fat: 17.1g	Protein: 18g

Dessert

181.   Sesame Seeds Cookies

Preparation time: 15 minutes   **Cooking time:** 10 minutes   **Servings:** 8

Ingredients:

- 1 cup almond flour
- 2 tablespoons coconut shred
- 2 eggs, beaten
- 1 teaspoon baking powder
- ¼ cup Splenda
- 3 tablespoons sesame seeds
- 1 tablespoon coconut oil, softened

Directions:

1. Set all ingredients in the mixing bowl and knead the dough.
2. Make the balls from the dough and press them gently in the shape of the cookies.
3. Set the cookies in the air fryer basket in one layer and cook them for 10 minutes at 360F.

Nutrition:

Calories: 177

Fat: 12.4g

Fiber: 2.2g

Carbohydrates: 10.7g

Protein: 5g

182.   Walnut Bars

Preparation time: 15 minutes   **Cooking time:** 16 minutes   **Servings:** 4

Ingredients:

- 1 egg, beaten
- 2 tablespoons Erythritol
- 7 tablespoons coconut oil, softened
- 1 teaspoon vanilla extract
- ¼ cup coconut flour
- 1 oz. walnuts, chopped
- ½ teaspoon baking powder

Directions:

1. Mix egg with Erythritol, coconut oil, vanilla extract, coconut flour, and baking powder.
2. Stir the mixture gently, add walnuts, and mix the mixture until homogenous.
3. Set the mixture in the air fryer basket and flatten gently.
4. Cook the walnut bars at 375F for 16 minutes.
5. Cool the dessert well and cut into bars.

Nutrition:

Calories: 298

Fat: 29.8g

Fiber: 3.5g

Carbohydrates: 6.2g

Protein: 4.1g

183.   Blondies

Preparation time: 10 minutes   **Cooking time:** 15 minutes   **Servings:** 2

Ingredients:

- 1 egg, beaten
- 1 tablespoon almond butter
- ½ teaspoon baking powder
- 1 teaspoon lime juice
- ½ teaspoon vanilla extract
- 1 teaspoon Splenda
- 2 tablespoons almond flour

Directions:

1. Set all ingredients in the mixer bowl and mix until smooth.
2. Pour Set mixture in the air fryer basket, flatten gently, and cook at 375F for 15 minutes.
3. Then cut the cooked dessert into servings.

Nutrition:

Calories: 138

Fat: 10.1g

Fiber: 1.6g

Carbohydrates: 6.4g

Protein: 6g

184.   Chocolate Cream

Preparation time: 10 minutes   **Cooking time:** 15 minutes   **Servings:** 3
Ingredients:

- 1 oz. dark chocolate, chopped
- 1 cup coconut cream
- 1 teaspoon vanilla extract
- 1 tablespoon Erythritol

Directions:

1. Pour coconut cream in the air fryer.
2. Add chocolate, vanilla extract, and Erythritol.
3. Cook the chocolate cream for 15 minutes at 360F. Stir the liquid from time to time during cooking.

Nutrition:
Calories: 236
Fat: 21.9g
Fiber: 2g
Carbohydrates: 10.3g
Protein: 2.6g

185.   Pecan Nutella

Preparation time: 20 minutes   **Cooking time:** 5 minutes   **Servings:** 4
Ingredients:

- 4 pecans, chopped
- 5 teaspoons butter, softened
- ½ teaspoon vanilla extract
- 1 tablespoon Splenda
- 1 teaspoon of cocoa powder

Directions:

1. Put all ingredients in the air fryer and stir gently.
2. Cook the mixture at 400F for 5 minutes.
3. Then transfer the mixture in the serving bowl and refrigerate for 15-20 minutes before serving.

Nutrition:
Calories: 157
Fat: 14.8g
Fiber: 1.6g
Carbohydrates: 5.3g
Protein: 1.6g

186.   Ricotta Cookies

Preparation time: 15 minutes   **Cooking time:** 12 minutes   **Servings:** 6
Ingredients:

- 1 teaspoon vanilla extract
- 1 cup ricotta cheese
- 1 cup coconut flour
- 1 egg, beaten
- 2 tablespoons swerve

Directions:

1. Mix coconut flour with vanilla extract, ricotta cheese, egg, and swerve.
2. Knead the dough and make cookies.
3. Put the cookies in the air fryer and cook at 365F for 12 minutes.

Nutrition:
Calories: 150
Fat: 6g
Fiber: 8g
Carbohydrates: 15.6g
Protein: 8.3g

187.   Cream Cheese Pie

Preparation time: 15 minutes   **Cooking time:** 30 minutes   **Servings:** 6
Ingredients:

- 2 eggs, beaten
- 6 tablespoons almond flour
- ½ teaspoon vanilla extract
- 6 tablespoons cream cheese
- ½ teaspoon baking powder
- 1 teaspoon apple cider vinegar
- ½ teaspoon ground cinnamon
- 3 tablespoons Erythritol
- 1 tablespoon coconut oil, melted

Directions:

1. Brush the baking pan with coconut oil.

2. Then mix eggs with almond flour, vanilla extract, cream cheese, baking powder, apple cider vinegar, ground cinnamon, and Erythritol.
3. Merge the mixture until smooth and pour it in the baking pan.
4. Cook the pie in the air fryer at 350F for 30 minutes.
5. Then cool the cooked pie well.

Nutrition:

Calories: 120

Fat: 10.6g

Fiber: 0.9g

Carbohydrates: 2.3g

Protein: 4.1g

188.   Greece Style Cake

Preparation time: 10 minutes   **Cooking time:** 30 minutes   **Servings:** 12

Ingredients:

- 6 eggs, beaten
- 1 teaspoon vanilla extract
- 1 teaspoon baking powder
- 2 cups almond flour
- 4 tablespoons Erythritol
- 1 cup Plain yogurt

Directions:

1. Mix all ingredients in the mixing bowl.
2. Then pour the mixture in the air fryer and flatten it gently.
3. Cook the cake at 350F for 30 minutes.

Nutrition:

Calories: 159

Fat: 11.3g

Fiber: 2g

Carbohydrates: 5.9g

Protein: 7.9g

189.   Pecan Cobbler

Preparation time: 15 minutes   **Cooking time:** 30 minutes   **Servings:** 4

Ingredients:

- ¼ cup coconut cream
- 1 egg, beaten
- ½ cup coconut flour
- 1 teaspoon vanilla extract
- 2 tablespoons coconut oil, softened
- 3 pecans, chopped

Directions:

1. Mix coconut oil with pecans and put the mixture in the air fryer. Flatten the mixture gently.
2. In the mixing bowl, mix coconut cream with egg, coconut flour, and vanilla extract.
3. Put the mixture over the pecans, flatten it gently and cook at 350F for 30 minutes.
4. Cool the cooked meal and transfer in the plates.

Nutrition:

Calories: 245

Fat: 20.5g

Fiber: 7.5g

Carbohydrates: 12.5g

Protein: 4.8g

190.   Cocoa Pudding

Preparation time: 10 minutes   **Cooking time:** 20 minutes   **Servings:** 8

Ingredients:

- 2 cups ricotta cheese
- 2 tablespoons coconut flour
- 3 tablespoons Splenda
- 3 eggs, beaten
- 1 tablespoon vanilla extract
- ½ cup coconut cream
- 1 tablespoon cocoa powder

Directions:

1. Whisk the coconut cream with cocoa powder.
2. Then add eggs, Splenda, ricotta cheese, and coconut flour.
3. Mix the mixture until smooth and pour in the air fryer.
4. Cook the pudding at 350F for 20 minutes. Stir the pudding every 5 minutes during cooking.

Nutrition:

Calories: 180

Fat: 10.4g

Fiber: 1.3g

Carbohydrates: 10.5g

Protein: 9.9g

191. Lemon Biscotti

Preparation time: 15 minutes **Cooking time:** 40 minutes **Servings:** 6

Ingredients:

- 2 oz. almonds, chopped
- 2 tablespoons coconut oil
- 2 eggs, beaten
- 1 teaspoon vanilla extract
- 1 cup coconut flour
- 1 teaspoon lemon zest, grated
- ½ teaspoon baking powder
- 1 teaspoon lemon juice
- ¼ cup coconut cream
- 1 teaspoon sesame oil
- 3 tablespoons Erythritol

Directions:

1. Mix all ingredients in the mixing bowl.
2. Then knead the dough and put in the air fryer basket.
3. Cook the dough for 38 minutes at 375F.
4. Then slice the dough into biscotti and cook at 400F for 2 minutes more.

Nutrition:

Calories: 227

Fat: 15.9g

Fiber: 9.4g

Carbs: 16.4g

Protein: 6.8g

192. Chia Pie

Preparation time: 10 minutes **Cooking time:** 30 minutes **Servings:** 8

Ingredients:

- 1 cup almond flour
- 2 tablespoons chia seeds
- 4 eggs, beaten
- 4 tablespoons Erythritol
- 1 teaspoon vanilla extract
- 2 tablespoons coconut oil, melted

Directions:

1. Brush the air fryer basket with coconut oil.
2. Then mix almond flour with chia seeds, eggs, vanilla extract, and Erythritol.
3. Put the mixture in the air fryer basket, flatten it in the shape of the pie and cook at 365F for 30 minutes.

Nutrition:

Calories: 164

Fat: 13.3

Fiber: 2.7

Carbohydrates 4.7

Protein: 6.4

193. Ricotta Muffins

Preparation time: 15 minutes **Cooking time:** 11 minutes **Servings:** 4

Ingredients:

- 4 teaspoons ricotta cheese
- 1 egg, beaten
- ½ teaspoon baking powder
- 1 teaspoon vanilla extract
- 8 teaspoons coconut flour
- 3 tablespoons coconut cream
- 2 teaspoons Erythritol
- Cooking spray

Directions:

1. Spray the muffin molds with cooking spray.
2. Then mix all ingredients in the mixing bowl.
3. When you get a smooth batter, pour it in the muffin molds and place in the air fryer basket.
4. Cook the muffins at 365F for 11 minutes.

Nutrition:

Calories: 72

Fat: 4.7g

Fiber: 2.3g

Carbohydrates: 4.7g

Protein: 2.9g

194. Sweet Baked Avocado

Preparation time: 5 minutes   **Cooking time:** 20 minutes   **Servings:** 2

Ingredients:

- 1 avocado, pitted, halved
- 2 teaspoons Erythritol
- 1 teaspoon vanilla extract
- 2 teaspoons butter

Directions:

1. Sprinkle the avocado halves with Erythritol, vanilla extract, and butter.
2. Put the avocado halves in the air fryer and cook at 350F for 20 minutes.

Nutrition:

Calories: 245

Fat: 23.4g

Fiber: 6.7g

Carbohydrates: 8.9g

Protein: 2g

195. Rhubarb Pie

Preparation time: 15 minutes   **Cooking time:** 20 minutes   **Servings:** 6

Ingredients:

- 4 oz. rhubarb, chopped
- ¼ cup coconut cream
- 1 teaspoon vanilla extract
- ¼ cup Erythritol
- 1 cup coconut flour
- 1 egg, beaten
- 4 tablespoons coconut oil, softened

Directions:

1. Mix coconut cream with vanilla extract, Erythritol, coconut flour, egg, and coconut oil.
2. When the mixture is smooth, add rhubarb and stir gently.
3. Pour the mixture in the air fryer and cook the pie at 375F for 20 minutes.
4. Cool the cooked pie and cut into servings.

Nutrition:

Calories: 198

Fat: 14.2g

Fiber: 8.6g

Carbohydrates: 14.9g

Protein: 4g

196. Lemon Pie

Preparation time: 10 minutes   **Cooking time:** 35 minutes   **Servings:** 6

Ingredients:

- 1 cup coconut flour
- ½ lemon, sliced
- ¼ cup heavy cream
- 2 eggs, beaten
- 2 tablespoons Erythritol
- 1 teaspoon baking powder
- Cooking spray

Directions:

1. Set the air fryer basket with cooking spray.
2. Then line the bottom of the air fryer with lemon.
3. In the mixing bowl, mix coconut flour with heavy cream, eggs, Erythritol, and baking powder.
4. Pour the batter over the lemons and cook the pie at 365F for 35 minutes.

Nutrition:

Calories: 120

Fat: 5.3g

Fiber: 8.2g

Carbs: 4.4g

Protein: 4.7g

197. Sponge Cake

Preparation time: 10 minutes   **Cooking time:** 30 minutes   **Servings:** 6

Ingredients:

- 2 cups coconut flour
- 5 eggs, beaten
- ½ cup Erythritol
- 1 teaspoon baking powder
- 1 teaspoon vanilla extract
- Cooking spray

Directions:

1. Whisk the coconut flour with eggs, Erythritol, baking powder, and vanilla extract.
2. Set the baking pan with cooking spray and pour the coconut flour mixture inside.
3. Put the pan in the air fryer basket and cook at 355F for 30 minutes.

Nutrition:

Calories: 75

Fat: 4.3g

Fiber: 1.7g

Carbs: 3.4g

Protein: 5.3g

198.   Baked Cantaloupe

Preparation time: 10 minutes   **Cooking time:** 10 minutes   **Servings:** 2

Ingredients:

- 1 cup cantaloupe, chopped
- 1 teaspoon vanilla extract
- 1 tablespoon Erythritol
- 1 teaspoon olive oil

Directions:

1. Put the cantaloupe in the air fryer basket and sprinkle with vanilla extract, Erythritol, and olive oil.
2. Cook the dessert at 375F for 10 minutes.

Nutrition:

Calories: 53

Fat: 2.5g

Fiber: 0.7g

Carbohydrates: 6.6g

Protein: 0.7g

199.   Sweet Carrabolla Chips

Preparation time: 10 minutes   **Cooking time:** 50 minutes   **Servings:** 6

Ingredients:

- 10 oz. Carrabolla, sliced
- 1 teaspoon coconut oil, melted
- 1 tablespoon Erythritol

Directions:

1. Mix Carrabolla with coconut oil and Erythritol.
2. Then set it in the air fryer and cook at 340F for 50 minutes. Shake the carambola slices every 5 minutes.

Nutrition:

Calories: 21

Fat: 0.9g

Fiber: 1.3g

Carbohydrates: 3.2g

Protein: 0.5g

200.   Blueberries Muffins

Preparation time: 10 minutes   **Cooking time:** 20 minutes   **Servings:** 6

Ingredients:

- 2 teaspoons blueberries
- 1 teaspoon baking powder
- 4 tablespoons coconut flour
- 4 tablespoons coconut oil, softened
- 3 tablespoons Erythritol

Directions:

1. Set all ingredients in the mixing bowl and mix until smooth.
2. Then pour the mixture in the muffin molds.
3. Place the muffin molds in the air fryer basket and cook at 350F for 20 minutes.

Nutrition:

Calories: 100

Fat: 9.6g

Fiber: 2g

Carbs: 9.9g

Protein: 0.7g

Measurement Conversion Chart

VOLUME EQUIVALENTS(DRY)

US STANDARD	METRIC (APPROXIMATE)
1/8 teaspoon	0.5 mL
1/4 teaspoon	1 mL
1/2 teaspoon	2 mL
3/4 teaspoon	4 mL
1 teaspoon	5 mL
1 tablespoon	15 mL
1/4 cup	59 mL
1/2 cup	118 mL
3/4 cup	177 mL
1 cup	235 mL
2 cups	475 mL
3 cups	700 mL
4 cups	1 L

VOLUME EQUIVALENTS(LIQUID)

US STANDARD	US STANDARD (OUNCES)	METRIC (APPROXIMATE)
2 tablespoons	1 fl.oz.	30 mL
1/4 cup	2 fl.oz.	60 mL
1/2 cup	4 fl.oz.	120 mL
1 cup	8 fl.oz.	240 mL
1 1/2 cup	12 fl.oz.	355 mL
2 cups or 1 pint	16 fl.oz.	475 mL
4 cups or 1 quart	32 fl.oz.	1 L
1 gallon	128 fl.oz.	4 L

TEMPERATURES EQUIVALENTS

FAHRENHEIT(F)	CELSIUS(C) (APPROXIMATE)
225 °F	107 °C
250 °F	120 °C
275 °F	135 °C
300 °F	150 °C
325 °F	160 °C
350 °F	180 °C
375 °F	190 °C
400 °F	205 °C
425 °F	220 °C
450 °F	235 °C
475 °F	245 °C
500 °F	260 °C

WEIGHT EQUIVALENTS

US STANDARD	METRIC (APPROXIMATE)
1 ounce	28 g
2 ounces	57 g
5 ounces	142 g
10 ounces	284 g
15 ounces	425 g
16 ounces	455 g
(1 pound)	
1.5 pounds	680 g
2 pounds	907 g

Index

Conclusion

The Air Fryer is one of the best device you can buy. It is easy to use and very well-constructed. It offers so many benefits that it would be worth it for anyone looking to buy an air fryer for their home. You will be able to economize money and get healthier food to eat. It lets you cook your favorite meals with little effort and can do all types of cooking. It comes with many helpful features that make cooking a breeze. It can replace the need for many other appliances and is very versatile.

If you are digging for an air fryer that allows you to cook various foods healthily, this would be perfect for you. You will be able to adore all your favorite meals and snacks at home too. This would be worth having if you are looking for one on sale or cheap.

If you are looking for a new way of dieting, this may be a good choice. It would allow you to eat the foods you love while still maintaining your weight and being healthy. You will not have to give up your favorite foods so that you can stay healthy and fit. You will be able to get healthier food choices that are much tastier and more filling than what you eat from fast-food restaurants or other stores. It is a great way to stay healthy and enjoy the foods you love. It is very easy to use and can be used by anyone. It can cook a variety of foods in little time to not have to spend all day cooking. It is also very well-constructed so that it will last for many years without needing repairs or replacements. You will be able to make your favorite dishes from home that your family and friends will enjoy as well.

The recipes included in the guidebook will help you get started and give you a good idea of how Air Fryer works. If you are seeking for a healthy way to cook your favorite foods, this cookbook is a great buy.

Printed in Great Britain
by Amazon

84751676R00054